D1738124

THE SUMERIANS

EARLY CULTURE SERIES

Series Editor: Edward R. Sammis

Historical Adviser: C. C. Lamberg-Karlovsky

Professor of Anthropology, Curator of Near Eastern Archaeology, Harvard University

The ⟞⟶ SUMERIANS

Inventors and Builders

Elizabeth Lansing

Illustrated in black and white and full color

McGRAW-HILL BOOK COMPANY

New York • St. Louis • San Francisco • Toronto

Note: Except where specifically indicated, the translations of poems and epics in this book have been taken from *The Sumerians,* by Samuel N. Kramer.

Contents

Introduction

THE past one hundred years
have seen archaeology move from an interest in "antiquarian
curios," objects fashioned in the past by unknown peoples and
cultures, to a complex science which brings together the archaeologist, physicist, chemist, geologist, botanist, and others.
They have one goal: understanding man's past, his ever-changing environment, and the cultural processes which led him from
the past to the present. Today archaeological research is pro-
gressing rapidly, giving us results in an ever-changing view of
man's past. Thus, just as the biological sciences are continually
altering man's view of his present, so archaeology adds to and
changes our conception of man's evolution.

The archaeologist through his recent excavations and discoveries provides a "Progress Report," not only in the understanding of our past but in its relevance to the present and
future. The next spade of earth uncovered on a dig, or text
translated by a linguist, or perhaps even chemist's analysis of
a metal object of prehistoric date, may well subject this "Progress Report" to a major change in our own understanding of
man's earlier accomplishments.

7

There are today several excavations which are shedding new light on the Sumerians. I have myself been excavating a site, Tepe Yahya in southeastern Iran, which has added substantially to our understanding of the economic relations between Iran and Mesopotamia at the time of the Sumerians. The author of this volume introduces the reader to Sargon and Naram-Sin, powerful kings of the late third millennium empire of the Akkadians. We have known from texts that both of these men opened trade relations with peoples occupying the Indus Valley. With the excavation of our own site we have been able to establish material evidence of the trade relations which existed between these earliest and largest of civilizations. Through such work we can reach a better understanding of the early economic relations which existed then.

The reader of this book will note that the Sumerians have had to deal with problems broadly similar to those now confronting us: problems resulting from major technological innovations and discoveries which, then as now, had profound effects on human culture. Just as the present-day use of the computer has "revolutionized" our society, so did the introduction and invention of writing and metallurgy and the beginning of urban life revolutionize life among the Sumerians—the impact of which we still live with today. From an understanding of these earlier "revolutions" we may be able to discern parallels between them and our own situation.

The author of this book is to be congratulated for providing a stimulating "Progress Report" on that most important of man's ventures or confrontations—civilization. The Sumerians, brought to life in this book, represent man's first successful adaptation to and adoption of complex legal systems, political organization, and religious beliefs as well as educational institutions and economic patterns. These are discussed not only in light of the literary evidences from the texts but also of archaeological excavations.

It has been often said that the archaeologist's aim is to show the fundamental continuity of man's past with the present: in effect, to show his ups and downs in the slow progress from barbarism to civilization. The reader of this book will be struck by the "Stranger in Nippur" (Chapter 4) and see in him not the separate body of tedious chronological detail relating to another world, so often associated with historical and archaeological writing, but a "stranger" who is strangely familiar to us, engaging in a task which is wholly understandable to us in the here and now.

The reader will set this book down with a new appreciation, perhaps even wonder, revealed by the panorama of Sumerian civilization, and its technological and aesthetic contribution, for which we may today be thankful—as its heirs. The "Progress Report" which follows represents a fine appreciation of the Sumerian gift—a civilization uncovered by archaeologists only in this century after over four thousand years of silence.

C.C. Lamberg-Karlovsky
Professor of Anthropology
Curator of Near Eastern Archaeology
Harvard University

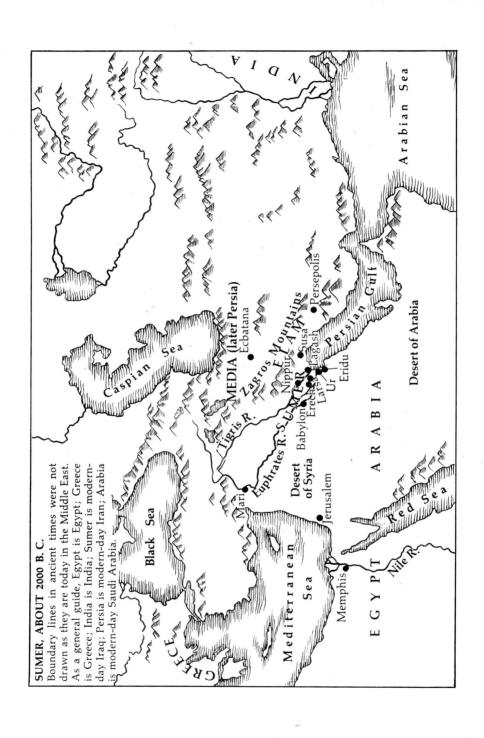

SUMER, ABOUT 2000 B. C.
Boundary lines in ancient times were not drawn as they are today in the Middle East. As a general guide, Egypt is Egypt; Greece is Greece; India is India; Sumer is modern-day Iraq; Persia is modern-day Iran; Arabia is modern-day Saudi Arabia.

INDIA

Arabian Sea

Caspian Sea

MEDIA (later Persia)

Persepolis

Ecbatana

ELAM

Zagros Mountains

Susa

Persian Gulf

Nippur

Lagash

S U M E R

Tigris R.

Larsa

Ur

Eridu

Euphrates R.

Erech

Babylon

A R A B I A

Desert of Arabia

Mari

Desert of Syria

Jerusalem

Black Sea

Mediterranean Sea

GREECE

Red Sea

E G Y P T

Memphis

Nile R.

chapter 1

A LOST WORLD

EARLY in 1850 two young Englishmen rode out from Babylon in search of a lost world. Their horses plodded eastward across a vast sea of burning sand, for this lower region of Mesopotamia, which is now called Iraq, was a barren land deserted by history for nearly two thousand years. Many thousands of people had lived in what was known as the Land between the Rivers. Now the only humans in this narrow strip lying between the Tigris and the Euphrates were occasional tribes of Bedouin nomads who pitched their tents near the crumbled ruins of long-dead cities.

Henry Loftus and his companion, Harry Churchill, were members of a British commission which had come to the Middle East to help settle a boundary dispute between Persia and Turkey. Loftus was a geologist who had joined the commission in London so that he might study the rock formations of this ancient area. But his imagination had been fired by the mounds of broken brick and the massive remains of the Tower of Babel he had seen in Babylon. He had heard exciting rumors of even older ruins to the south at the head of the Persian Gulf, and he meant to be the first European to explore them. Harry Churchill was a man with an equally adventurous spirit. They

12

Ziggurat (temple) to Inanna the goddess of love, at Erech.

got permission from the leader of the British commission to strike out on their own with only a small party of bearers.

The caravan moved slowly "across a level and sandy desert, intersected by an infinity of ancient irrigation canals." The account Churchill wrote of his journey tells that "Now and then a low mound and a few fragments of pottery, bricks and glass [told] of the former inhabitants of the land. . . ." Behind the two horsemen straggled the train of pack mules and Arab bearers, carrying the tents, food, and equipment needed for the expedition. The Arabs muttered among themselves, obviously puzzled by the madness of these foreigners who had come to disturb the dust of their desert land. What did Loftus hope to find on this deserted plain? Why did he think he might uncover evidence of a civilization older than that of Babylon and Nineveh?

Long before Loftus set out on his journey into the past, even as early as the twelfth century, excavators had been at work among the ruins in northern Mesopotamia. The cities of Babylon and Nineveh, located near Baghdad and Mosul, were accessible to investigation. Early diggers found thousands upon thousands of broken tablets inscribed with wedge-shaped markings. In the nineteenth century, however, the period when really active excavation began, men were trying to find confirmation that Babylon had indeed been destroyed "by God's wrath," as the Old Testament stated. These markings, therefore, did not interest the early explorers nearly as much as the realization that they were digging into biblical history.

"Woe to the bloody city!" cried the prophet Nahum. ". . . Thy shepherds slumber, O king of Assyria; thy nobles shall dwell in the dust; thy people is scattered upon the mountain." In the sand and rubble of old Babylon the excavators found charred bricks which they felt were proof that a great conflagration had once reduced this proud city to dust. The crumbled mass of tiered stones was identified as the famed Tower of

King Sargon II with two courtiers at the palace of Khorsabad. Louvre.

Babel in Babylon and the remnants of palaces were those of Nebuchadnezzar, who carried the children of Israel into captivity. Bits and pieces of stone, along with brick and delicately carved stone cylinder seals, were brought back to Europe. Larger sculptures were sent to museums in London and Paris. It was easy to imagine that the heavily bearded stone faces with their bulging eyes and grim jaws were representations of those dreaded Assyrian kings Sennacherib and Nebuchadnezzar.

Inspired by curiosity and perhaps greediness, the great museums of Europe sent expeditions on a vast treasure hunt. They had orders to bring back further evidence of those kings and conflagrations to which the Bible bore such violent witness. These early excavators made some significant discoveries. A French expedition unearthed the palace of the Assyrian king Sargon II at Khorsabad and also discovered a magnificent array of huge sculptures, which were carried back to the Louvre. Men from the British Museum explored the ruins of Nimrud and Nineveh. Digging into the massive heaps of sand, they unearthed the palaces of Ashurbanipal and Sennacherib at Nineveh.

The prophet Isaiah had promised that the Lord would "put a blast upon him [Sennacherib] . . . and will cause him to fall by the sword in his own land." Isaiah's prophecy was fulfilled when Sennacherib was murdered in 681 B.C. by his own sons. But before his death, the monarch collected a royal library of some 32,000 tablets, which were found in the rubble of his palace. The "Lion Hunt" sculptures, the glazed bricks and delicate bits of gold jewelry which the British Museum got from these "digs" satisfied the English that they weren't being outdone by the French.

By the middle of the nineteenth century those 32,000 baked-clay tablets were suddenly of far more interest to scholars than the stone faces of biblical kings. The mysterious wedge-shaped characters which earlier explorers had looked upon as "decorations" were accepted as some sort of written record. They were given the name cuneiform because of their triangular shapes. Some translations had been made and scholars suspected that the history of a lost civilization was written on those baked-clay tablets.

The legends, myths, trade agreements, laws, and literature of an ancient people gradually came to light. The tablets spoke of cities—Erech, Ur, Ellasar—that had been lost to history since the time of Abraham.

The Book of Genesis says, ". . . as they journeyed from the

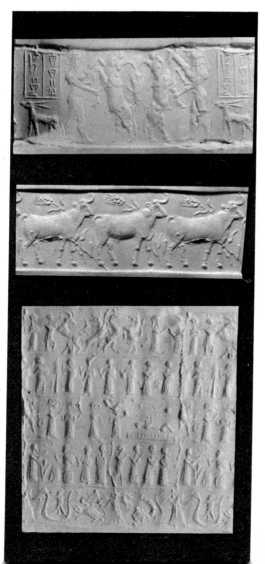

Impressions made by small cylinder seals show detailed workmanship and familiar scenes. Louvre.

Head of woman found near Erech. Museum of Baghdad.

east, they found a plain in the land of Shinar; and they dwelt there."

Henry Loftus had high hopes, when he and Churchill set out in 1850, that the lost land of Shinar lay somewhere in that vast plain to the south. With the temperature often reaching 104 degrees Fahrenheit, they made a slow journey southward. Along the way, they made haphazard digs at some of the mounds of sand and rubble, only to find that these sites had been plundered over the centuries by local graverobbers, looking for gold and precious stones. Such treasures had long ago been carried off to be sold in the bazaars of Baghdad. But the broken pots and inscribed tablets, which had no saleable value, fortunately had been left behind.

Loftus had no way of identifying any of the massive sand heaps they encountered as the remains of a particular city. But he knew that if his journey was to have any significance, he must bring back some inscribed pots or tablets. A cuneiform scholar, in translating the wedge-shaped markings, might come upon the name of one of the ancient cities mentioned in the Bible, proof that this area was indeed the plain in the land of Shinar.

The Arabs whom Loftus met along the way maintained that a settlement called Warka at the head of the Persian Gulf was near the site of ancient Erech, a city named in the Bible. When they reached Warka, Loftus and Churchill saw a huge heap of ruins, almost completely buried in sand. No one, with the exception of Arab treasure-seekers, had made any attempt to dig into it. Loftus and Churchill, aided by the Arabs, scoured the ruins for three months. At last, they mapped out "an irregular circle, nearly six miles in circumference, defined by traces of an earthen rampart, in some places fifty feet high." Somewhere in this mass of broken pottery and rubble Loftus hoped to find a tablet or pot inscribed with the magic name "Erech."

He was especially interested in obtaining an unbroken baked-clay burial urn, for these huge pots were covered with cuneiform script. But, as he wrote, "they invariably fell into pieces in the attempt to stir them. After several days of anxious labor and the demolition of perhaps a hundred pots, I almost despaired of success. The Arabs were anxious that I should be pleased [and] at last the good-natured Guza [an Arab workman] took hold of my sleeve and addressed me . . . 'Oh, Beg [master], you take much trouble to get one of these pots of the old *Kaffirs* [a non-Moslem] and have brought spades and shovels from a great distance for this purpose. . . . Give us your permission, Beg, and we shall follow our own mode of search. . . .'"

The Arabs had only their spears for implements. Digging with these, they soon found an unbroken urn with enough cuneiform markings to serve Loftus' purpose. He prepared for his journey home, but his troubles were not altogether over.

The Arabs carried the urn slung between two long poles. Balancing the poles on one shoulder, they held their ever-present spears in their free hands. The pot had once held the ashes of a departed human being and the Arab bearers couldn't resist the temptation to make a funeral march of the trip. The importance of their burden and their fine sense of drama made the journey precarious, both for the pot and for Loftus' nerves.

(Above.) This figure of a
woman in terracotta is a
goddess symbol from Ur.
British Museum.
(Below.) Man fashioned
of copper is a
worshipper. Chicago,
Oriental Institute,
Museum of the
University.

Excavation at Larsa shows foundation of the city's buildings which
rose on the desert in 3000 BC.

All along the dusty miles the Arabs sang and danced, brandish-
ing their spears and shouting defiance at imaginary enemies.

Occasionally they met a group of nomads who challenged
them with pretended assaults. Exchanging shouts, insults, and
cries of triumph, the Arabs charged one another amid a forest
of waving spears. The nomad women joined the fracas, wailing
for the ashes of the departed and throwing dust into their hair
in the ancient ceremony of mourning.

During this lively journey Loftus never took his eyes from
the precious pot. By some miracle it still rode safe in the
sling. "At last," he wrote, "we came safely to Babylon."

Loftus was as lucky as he was daring. One of the bits of baked clay he brought back to England was inscribed with the magic word "Erech." For the first time scholars had proof that the old biblical cities did lie beneath the sand mounds on the plains of Shinar in southern Mesopotamia.

Soon after Loftus' journey, a new spirit of scientific inquiry began to motivate diggings and explorations. Darwin's *Origin of Species,* published in 1859, had thoroughly upset the old ideas of biblical history. The men who now came to probe into the past were not primarily concerned with proving a theory or acquiring prizes for museums. They were archaeologists, men who set out with open minds to try to discover, by digging and study, who the ancient peoples were and how they lived.

In the next fifty years a number of other sand heaps on that southern plain were partially uncovered. Among them were Ellasar, which the Sumerians called Larsa; Ur, where Abraham was born; and Eridu, at the mouth of the Euphrates. Many of these cities of the past were identified by the inscribed cylinders found in the cornerstones of crumbling walls. Here at last was dramatic evidence that a civilization far older than those of Babylon and Assyria had once existed in the area. Archaeologists realized that the Land of Shinar must have been the home of the Sumerians, for Sumer and Shinar were one and the same. A land lost for centuries was rising out of the sand. Thousands upon thousands of clay tablets were recovered, proving that the legends of Babylon and Nineveh had their origins in the tales of a far older civilization.

The deeper the archaeologists dug, the further they penetrated into history. But here was a history that kept no dates. All ancient peoples had used pottery for cooking, for storing food, and even for preserving the ashes of their dead. Each pot had its own special style and even the tiniest fragment of a broken jar told its own story of migration, invasion, fire or massacre. The style changed after such catastrophes, sometimes within a generation. The archaeologists were therefore able to develop their own system of establishing dates, based on the pots they found.

Working backward in history, a time chart was established that set dates for each "culture," a word that describes a people who made the same sort of pottery at a particular time. Digging down into the mounds at Erech, for instance, excavators found definite layers, or strata, which showed that the old city had been built up time and time again on the same site. In each instance, through some catastrophe or action of a natural force such as erosion or wind, portions of the city were destroyed. Each time a calamity occurred, the people had returned to build a new city upon the ruins of the old. Such strata were packed with bits of telltale pottery, each with its

own style.   After scholars had established dates defining these
layers of history, they could then compare them with the strata
in the ruins of another city where the same type of pottery had
been found.

The excavating itself was done with greater skill and care.
When a walled city fell into ruins, it tended to form a mass
of rubble.   Only a thin dark line remained to show where the
original walls had been.   As Loftus had done at Erech, excavators first traced the wall of the city limits before disturbing
the dust of the ruins.   Test pits were drilled down through each
mound.   When the drills hit virgin soil (earth undisturbed by
man), the excavators knew they had reached the beginning of
civilization at any given dig.

In the twentieth century archaeologists have tended to spe-
cialize in certain areas.   Those who were interested in Assyrian
and Babylonian history excavated at sites in the northern part
of Mesopotamia, leaving the Sumerian scholars to work amid
the sand heaps on the southern plain.

In 1922, an American expedition joined one from the British
Museum.   Excavations were begun at Ur, a city-state that had

Section of the excavation at Ur showing the strata
Woolley dug through.   1) level of the ruins 2) level
containing fragments of pottery 3) mud from the flood
4) ruins from before the flood 5) virgin soil 6) the
level of the sea

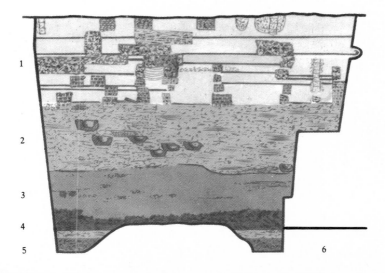

flourished at the height of Sumerian civilization. Sir Leonard
Woolley, an imaginative and enthusiastic British scholar, led
the expedition. His work and writing have inspired much of
the present-day interest in the history of Sumer.

At Ur, Sir Leonard uncovered the famous Death Pits. These
were the places where dozens of men and women apparently
"voluntarily" had died when a king or queen was buried. Here
were the bodies of the royal attendants who accompanied their
rulers to the next world. "The whole space . . . was crowded
with . . . men and women," wrote Sir Leonard, "while the
passage which led along the side of the stone [tomb] was lined
with soldiers carrying daggers. . . . On top of the bodies of the
'court ladies' . . . had been placed a wooden harp . . . by the

This game board, made of shell, bone, and lapis-lazuli, was found at
Ur. British Museum.

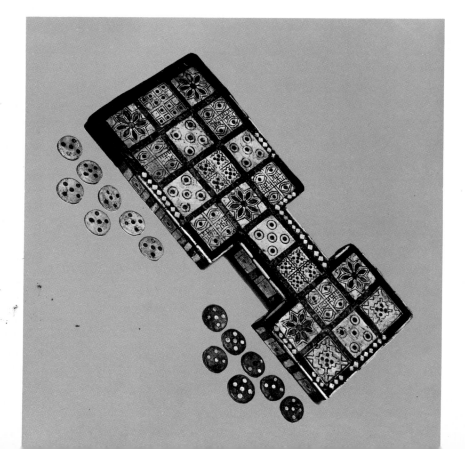

Sir Leonard and Lady Woolley often worked together during an
excavation.   Rev. H. Wooley.

side of the wall of the pit was a second harp, with a wonderful bull's head in gold, its eyes, beard and horn tips of lapis
lazuli. . . ."

"Nothing like such treasure had ever before come from the
soil of Mesopotamia," Sir Leonard declared.   The magnificence
of the golden helmets, bowls and lapis-lazuli jewelry "revealed
an art hitherto unsuspected and gave promise of future discoveries outstripping all hopes."

For twelve successive years Sir Leonard and his hordes of
native workmen labored in this fruitful mound of history.   His
books tell the fascinating story of his findings in their own vivid
way.   *Excavations at Ur* is the last of several, and each one
is a lively tale of adventure and discovery.

Digging into a small mound at al-Ubaid, not far from the
Death Pits, Sir Leonard found even more remarkable evidence
of how Sumerian history relates to biblical records.   "In the
year 1929 the work of excavating the Royal Cemetery at Ur

was drawing toward its end," he wrote. "The treasure recovered from its graves illustrated a civilization of an astonishingly high order and it was therefore all the more important to trace the steps by which man had reached that level of art and culture. That meant presumably we had to dig deeper."

The workmen sank a small shaft at al-Ubaid, digging through a mass of broken pottery and crumbled brick. Three feet down they reached a level of hard-packed mud, very like the virgin soil that in other digs marked the start of history and the end of further discovery. But Sir Leonard insisted the workmen keep on digging. A distance of three feet, he reasoned, could not extend very far into history. Also, he was curious about the quality of the virgin soil. Obviously it was water-laid mud, not the packed dust found at other sites.

He and Lady Woolley, who was as ardent a scholar as her husband, watched from the top of the five-foot-square shaft as the men dug down and down—six, eight, and ten feet. The Arabs no longer sang and shouted as they dug. Then, at last a workman's shovel turned up shards of green pottery and a few flint instruments. Eleven feet through that layer of silted dry mud they had reached civilization again. Sir Leonard wrote:

> I got into the pit once more, examined the sides, and by the time I had written up my notes . . . I wanted to see whether others would come to the same conclusion [about that layer of mud]. So, I brought up two of my staff and, pointing out the facts, asked for their explanation. They did not know what to say. My wife . . . was asked the same question, and she remarked casually, "Well, of course, it's the Flood."

chapter **2**

THE TURNING CENTURIES

. . . for seven days and seven nights,
The flood had swept over the land,
And the huge boat had been tossed about by
    the wind storms on the great waters . . .
Ziusudra opened a window on the huge
    boat. . . .

T HE man whose boat tossed on the great waters of the Flood was king of one of the city-states of Sumer. He reigned long before written history began. His name was Ziusudra. He was a good king, one who obeyed the gods in all things. Like Noah of the Bible, he was chosen to ride out the mighty deluge and thus preserve "the seed of mankind."

The story of this first "Noah" was found on a broken clay tablet in the ruins of Nippur. Only a third of the record remains and large parts are too blurred to make out. But the fragmentary words contain the first written account of the Flood. Centuries later when the Hebrew scholars wrote their version, Ziusudra had become Noah; and not only his family, but a whole zoo of paired animals, was deemed worthy of saving.

The Flood must have made a frightening impression on the people in the Land between the Rivers. Tales of its terrible destruction were handed down through generations. With each telling, the number of days increased and the waters grew deeper. Ziusudra's "huge boat" was "tossed about" for only "seven days and seven nights," while Noah and the Ark rode the Flood for forty days. But most scholars are of the opinion that it was the same Flood.

The bits of greenish pottery and the flint instruments which Sir Leonard found at al-Ubaid beneath those eleven feet of close-packed mud were however even more important to him than his dramatic proof that the Flood had really taken place. He was eager to "trace the steps" that led to the high order of Sumerian culture he had found at Ur. To him, the distinctive pottery was proof that people had lived on the Land between the Rivers before the deluge.

"Here at al-Ubaid," wrote Seton Lloyd, a distinguished student of the Middle East, "were people who appeared when the Gulf was beginning to recede. The silt brought down by the rivers was changing the sea into marshland and islands were beginning to appear . . . on which it was possible to live and plant corn."

Attracted by the enriched land, a nomad tribe, probably from the north in the Persian hills, decided "to live and plant corn" in the area about 5000 B.C. They built reed and mud huts with flat roofs and staircases leading up to them. Walls several feet high have been uncovered which must have once lined a tangle of narrow streets. The flint weapons and harpoons found in the rubble indicate that these people were hunters and fishermen as well as farmers.

Cup of stone with mother of pearl design, fashioned about 4000 BC. Museum of Damascus.

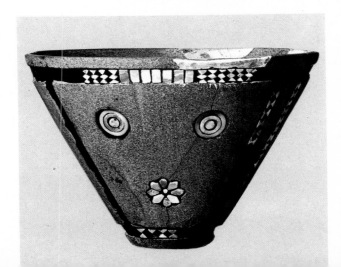

At a place called Uruk,* excavators found houses more sub-stantial than those at al-Ubaid. More important to scholars were the fragments of a reddish-black pottery with a highly polished surface. These shattered bits corresponded to the broken shards that Sir Leonard had come upon as he dug his way down to the Ubaid period (4500–3500 B.C.). The Uruk period (3500–3100 B.C.) comes after the Ubaid in the strata of history. Traces of the ancient culture at this time have been found in other digs throughout Iraq. These people used copper tools. Their buildings had arched doorways and were deco-rated with thousands of painted cones, pressed into a mosaic pattern, probably as a means of strengthening the walls.

But the peoples living during Uruk times left another legacy, far more important than their burnished pots and imaginative buildings. They were the first people to make written records. Crude clay tablets lay among the Uruk ruins, all of them marked with a simple pictograph sign. The marks were records of commercial dealings, noting the sales of goods or property. Curious cylinder seals were also used at this time as identifica-tion tags. These were stones approximately an inch long, each inscribed with a sign or picture that a man might press into a bit of damp clay and so make his mark. It was from these small beginnings that our art of communicating with one an-other through writing developed.

These early peoples were chiefly farmers and only inciden-tally potters, weavers, sculptors, fishermen, and builders. The cultivation of the wonderfully fertile soil was their reason for settling on the land. As their communities prospered, the Semitic wanderers of the surrounding deserts began to infiltrate their numbers. Some came peacefully and gradually inter-mingled with the established tillers of the soil. But others came intent on conquest and destruction. The Land between the Rivers had no natural boundaries. All during the centuries that

*Uruk is the Sumerian and Akkadian name for Erech.

preceded written history the agricultural settlements were regularly overrun by aggressive outsiders.

The early colonies were not destroyed and rebuilt overnight by successive groups of people. Long years may have passed before the people of the Uruk period, for instance, established themselves on the site where the people of the Ubaid period once lived. A natural catastrophe, such as a minor flood, may have destroyed the first Ubaid village. Perhaps a pestilence or an attack by a hostile tribe drove them from their firesides. Those who survived such a disaster may have been too few in number to regroup and gradually disappeared into the huge melting pot of the Middle East. The settlement they left behind crumbled into ruins. But this mound of rubble was valuable as real estate, because of its location near the life-giving river. Years or decades later, another tribe, building upon the same site, began a new stratum in history.

Traces of the Sumerians show up in the Land between the Rivers from approximately 3000 B.C. Whether they were native to the area or came from the outside is still being debated, although the most recent work indicates that they were probably native. Little is known of their culture at that time, but they must have been a highly imaginative and energetic people, for the area prospered after the arrival of the "black-headed people," as they called themselves. In the seven centuries from 2700 B.C. to 2000 B.C. that cover the high period of Sumerian civilization, this small and fertile crescent of land acquired wealth, political power, and a highly developed artistic and religious life.

A brief summary of their accomplishments, all of which are discussed later, shows clearly why the Sumerians are important in the development of our civilization. They were engineers who built irrigation canals to water the desert land. Since there was little stone available, they molded the river clay and baked bricks for building materials. From the same clay they made pots, jars, and even agricultural tools. They invented the wheel and used it for their pottery work, for wagons, and for military chariots. As architects, they used the arch and the dome. They devised a simple plow that is still in use today in the Middle East. They contributed sailboats that traveled great rivers and the waters of the eastern Mediterranean. They were accom-

A praying king of Mari, a Sumerian city on the Euphrates River. Museum of Damascus.

plished silversmiths, sculptors, and workers in bronze and copper.   But their finest achievement, their chief legacy to succeeding generations, was the invention of writing.

Written history begins with the Sumerian King Lists.   These lists of unpronounceable and largely forgotten names were found in the remains of the old cities.   They were copied and re-copied by scribes throughout the centuries.   Very few of the kings can be related to events and people that we can trace, for these ancient historians had no system for dating their documents.   They named the years in honor of some political or religious happening and fitted the kings into these events.

One such King List reports that "after the Flood had swept over [the land] and kingship descended from heaven, Kish became the seat of kingship."   By 2700 B.C. the settlements at the head of the Persian Gulf had grown into a group of city-states, each one ruled by a leader whose name appears on the King List.   Ur, Lagash, Kish, and Erech were walled cities

This beautifully etched silver vase shows an eagle, a lion, and a fawn.   Louvre.

where as many as a quarter of a million people lived. The names and dates of the different rulers are a puzzle to all but the experts in Sumerian history. Only a few stand out as kings of consequence, though our records are incomplete.

Etana, thirteenth of the Kings of Kish, probably ruled over much of Sumer early in the development of the "black-headed people" as a group with one culture. Documents refer to him as "he who stabilized the land." He must have been the first ruler who tried to bring the early agricultural settlements together as a nation. Clearly, his great success as an empire builder brought him widespread fame. Later myths claim that he was the man who "ascended to heaven."

Enmerkar was the first important king in Erech. He embarked on foreign conquest and, according to the epic tales, subjugated Aratta in what is now northern Iran. The fact that a king was made the hero of a myth or epic fixes him more surely in history than the mere mention of his name on a King List. Lugalbanda seems to have been just such a king, for he is the hero of at least two epic tales. His chief claim to fame, however, is that he was the grandfather of the mighty Gilgamesh.

Gilgamesh, who reigned about 2600 B.C., was a Hercules-Galahad-Paul Bunyan all rolled into one legendary figure. He was the greatest hero of Sumerian folklore. Tales of his mighty

This cuneiform tablet is an early Sumerian King List. British Museum.

deeds were written and repeated, not only by the Sumerians, but by other people of the ancient Middle East. Scholars weren't quite sure whether Gilgamesh was a man or a myth until a document found at Nippur was translated. In this Nippur text however he takes his place as a real king-hero who built a temple to the god Enlil. With no other contemporary records of his tremendous deeds, Gilgamesh lives most vividly in the myths and legends.

Beginning about 2500 B.C., the Lagash List gives a more or less unbroken line of kings over the next 150 years. One of the kings of Lagash, Eannatum, has left his name in history because of a boundary dispute between Lagash and the neighboring city of Umma. The Stele of the Vultures, a boundary stone found in the ruins of ancient Lagash, tells the story.

A quarrel between the two cities had been going on for years, long before Eannatum came to the throne. Both cities lay at the head of the Persian Gulf on the banks of the Tigris, and water rights were of paramount importance to them. Eannatum was determined to extend his rule over other city-states and, in order to be free to do so, he made a pact with Umma which granted each city certain rights to the river and canal waters. The Stele of the Vultures states that Enlil, the chief god of Sumer, "marked off the boundary . . . measured it off . . . and erected a stele there. . . . But Umma violated the decree of the god, ripped out the stele and entered the plain of Lagash."

Though Eannatum instantly made war on Umma for this heresy and "heaped up their skeleton piles on the plain," he was much too busy carrying his conquests to other areas to bother with the boundary dispute. His warriors were so successful he was able to assume the title King of Kish, which meant he was lord of Sumer, at least temporarily. As for the water rights dispute, it was neglected and not settled until a new canal was dug by Eannatum's successor.

But a new star was rising on the northern horizon. About 2400 B.C. the quarreling overlords of Sumer bowed to the rule

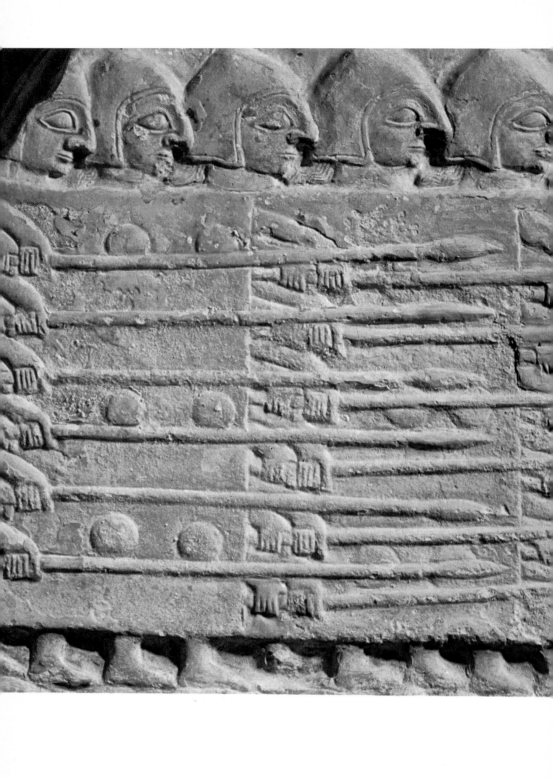

of the greatest king of them all, Sargon I, the Akkadian.   The
Akkadians were a Semitic-speaking people who had penetrated
into northern Mesopotamia and gradually subdued the entire
area.   The region called Akkad, where Sargon was born, lies
in the narrow belt of land where the two great rivers are only
twenty miles apart.

Sargon, like many of the world's conquerors, was a "man
of the people."   "My mother," he wrote, "was humble, I knew
not my father."   He goes on to say that his "mother . . . se-
cretly brought me to birth, set me in an ark of bulrushes . . .
consigned me to the river."   Later, by his own account, he was
rescued from this watery cradle by a "gardener" who "brought
me up to be his own son."   Then, "for fifty-four years the
kingship was mine."

Although the story of Sargon's childhood resembles that of
the biblical Moses, his later career took a more warlike course.
We know he began as a cupbearer to the lord of Kish.   But
Sargon's own story of his great conquests picks up the tale much
later when he was supreme ruler of all Sumer.   Inscriptions
recording his deeds have been found in the temple at Nippur.
They prove, as one historian says, that Sargon I was "the first
dynamic leader of men to emerge from the twilight of prehis-
tory into the full light of the written record. . . ."

Sargon became the leader of Kish and went on to subdue
Erech.   He brought its ruler in chains to the gates of Nippur,
which had already fallen before his chariots.   Divided by their
own jealousies and quarrels, the great city-states of Ur, Umma,
and Lagash were unable to band together and make a stand
against the all-conquering Sargon.   He vanquished them one
by one.

Sargon subdued the territories to the north as far as the
"Cedar Forest" and the "Silver Mountains," areas in the ranges

The soldiers of King Eannatum of Lagash march in victory in this
detail from the famous stele of the Vultures, about 3000 BC.   Louvre.

of the Taurus Mountains. With all of Mesopotamia in his power, he went on to foreign conquest and may even have made forays into Egypt, Ethiopia, and India. Contemporary legends are vague about the extent of his victories, but certainly much of the known world felt the horror of his "terrible, swift sword." Chariots, foot soldiers, and spearmen were organized into a vast army of conquest by the military and administrative genius of this former humble cupbearer.

Since his subjects were rebellious, Sargon stationed garrisons at key points in his empire, particularly in Sumer. He built himself a capital at Agade, near Kish, and established a city that became the most glorious in the known world. Sargon boasted that "5,400 men ate bread daily before him." His subject cities and provinces sent tribute from the "four quarters of the known world." Agade became a resplendent city, fit for one who was indeed "king of the world."

But even Sargon could not live forever. His sons who came after him had neither his military genius nor his administrative skill. The sprawling territories were in a constant state of upheaval as the conquered cities plotted and revolted against his sons and grandsons, who were hard put to hold the vast empire together.

One of Sargon's descendants, Naram-Sin, however, temporarily restored Agade to its former glory. But he made the mistake of sacking Nippur and defiling the sanctuary of its temple. According to legend, the supreme god, Enlil, to whom the temple was dedicated, avenged this desecration by calling upon the Gutians, ancient enemies of Sumer. *The Curse of Agade* tells in vivid poetic terms of the desolation of the once proud city.

Even the gods "turn their faces from the city," the epic relates, and "in not five days, not ten days" Enlil "lifted his eyes to the mountains and brought down the Gutians." They soon reduced Agade to such a state of misery that "the herald could not proceed on his journey, the sea-rider could not sail his boat . . . the land turned to clay. . . ." Famine stalked the countryside—"the great fields and meadows produce no grain, the fisheries produce no fish and the watered gardens produce neither honey nor wine."

For the next seven or eight decades the Gutians held Sumer in an uneasy bondage by balancing the powers of one city-state against another.   Lagash was evidently more friendly to its conquerors than other cities, for it gradually assumed more power under the Gutians.   This Lagash dynasty included Gudea, whose placid features were sculptured in countless statues found in the rubble of Lagash.   Gudea was a temple builder and must have had some power, for the records prove that he carried on trade in gold, cedar, and copper with countries as distant as Egypt and India.

The dreaded Gutians, "the snake, the scorpion, of the mountain," were driven off at last.   About 2050 B.C., Ur-Nammu, king of Ur, brought the surrounding cities under his control.   He created a cultural renaissance in Sumer, ushering in a golden age that lasted for nearly 150 years.   Under Ur-Nammu's enlightened rule literature and the arts flourished.   Trade increased and the science of astronomy developed.   Ur-Nammu built a great temple to the moon god, Nanna, a massive three-towered shrine that today is the finest example of Sumerian architecture yet uncovered on the plains of Mesopotamia.

But Sumer's star was falling.   By 2000 B.C. the Amorites from the west and the Elamites from the east had begun to overrun the rich cities along the great rivers.   The Sumerians were now no match for the tough fighters from the deserts and mountains.   For the next 250 years all of Sumer remained in a state of warfare and upheaval as successive city-states and kings struggled to maintain their hold on the Land between the Rivers.

Rulers rose and beat off the invaders, assuming some degree of power for a time.   But a small city in the center of the plain,

There are many statues of Gudea, ruler of Lagash. This one in diorite is inscribed. Louvre.

called Babylon, before now a place of little importance, was conquered by a vigorous warrior. His name was Hammurabi and by 1750 B.C. he had established Babylon as the supreme power in Sumer. The Sumerians themselves ceased to exist as a political and economic force. All their pomp and circumstance, their gold and glory were to lie buried for nearly 4,000 years. But they did leave behind in these ruins thousands upon thousands of clay tablets that give us valuable clues to the history of this once mighty people.

chapter **3**

MYSTERY OF THE WRITINGS

THE huge cliff towered 500 feet above the dusty road that led from Babylon to Kermanshah. High on its flat sunbaked surface, like a fly in a web, a man clung to the rock by a tangle of rope. The Persian and Kurdish workmen, clustered below in the blistering midday heat, had helped this strange Englishman build a scaffolding against the base of the Behistun Rock. They had even rigged the rope so he might come closer to the wedge-shaped marks and bas-reliefs (flat sculpture) that covered the massive face.

But only one of the workmen dared climb the fragile wooden structure. He was a mere boy, a young Kurd, agile as a cat. He had been the first to test the strength of the scaffold to show the tall, blue-eyed foreigner it was safe to climb. Now the Englishman himself was tied by a rope high above the scaffold and the boy was helping him press wads of wet paper into the rock surface. It was all incomprehensible to the watching Persians below, who no doubt thought it was very much against the will of Allah.

The man clinging to that high rock in the summer of 1835 was Henry Rawlinson. He was only twenty-five at the time and had already spent six years in the East as a member of the

Even today, archaeologists are studying the Behistun Rock. Note workman's rope hanging down the face. Courtesy George G. Cameron, the University of Michigan and The American Schools of Oriental Research.

East India Company, before joining the British armed forces in Persia. Rawlinson, like so many of his countrymen who had visited the area in the past century, was fascinated by the mysterious inscriptions he found there. Scholars recognized these symbols as those of long-dead languages, but so far very little progress had been made in translating them.

Before going on with Rawlinson's extraordinary efforts to make copies of the inscriptions on the Behistun Rock, it is necessary to mention something of the work less athletic scholars had already done to decipher the ancient writings. Why Rawlinson needed to have an accurate copy of the writing on the Behistun Rock is a complicated story, one that goes back into the earliest days of European interest in the ancient East.

In the first part of the seventeenth century, Pietro della Valle brought back to Europe the first inscribed brick from the mounds of Babylon. Ever since that time scholars had been puzzled by the wedge-shaped marks on its surface. Other

43

explorers and excavators in the following years had found more bricks, stones, and crumbled walls inscribed with the same strange symbols.

An especially impressive array of sculptures and inscriptions had been discovered at the site of Persepolis on the east side of the Persian Gulf. Travelers who went there as early as the sixteenth century knew that Persepolis had once been the ceremonial capital of those mighty Persian kings, Darius, Xerxes, and their heirs. Their dynasty had fought and flourished for 300 years until Alexander the Great destroyed Persepolis in 333 B.C. on his march to world conquest. Since then the ancient city had been left to the sand and sun. Mighty columns rose out of the desert; the walls of great palaces still stood amid the scattered stones of huge temples. These remains bore the same wedge-shaped writing and the sculptured figures of long-dead kings. Cut into the high cliffs surrounding the devastated city were elaborately decorated tombs where the Persian kings were buried. These, too, were covered with inscriptions of the same type.

A religious object inscribed in cuneiform and dedicated to the sun god. British Museum.

During the seventeenth and eighteenth centuries many learned arguments and literary battles were fought over these "characters of a strange and unusual shape." In 1700 an Englishman, Thomas Hyde, had given the characters the name cuneiform, a word derived from the Latin and meaning wedge-shaped. But Hyde maintained that the marks, which so often surrounded bas-reliefs of men and battles, were only decorations used to fill out the spaces around the stone carvings.

By the end of the eighteenth century fairly accurate copies of the Persepolis inscriptions had been made. The contending scholars were able to agree on one important point: the writings were recognized as trilingual, that is, they were written in three languages. For convenience, the writings were designated as Class I, Class II, and Class III.

Although it may seem a little involved, it is really important to know something about these three classes of writing. When scholars agreed that they represented three languages, they also discovered another interesting fact: the older a language is, the more characters it has. The very first written language was pictorial, that used by the people of the Uruk period. This ideographic form called for hundreds of symbols. Class III on the Persepolis stones had by far the most symbols and scholars realized it must therefore be the oldest. Class II had fewer forms and was a syllabic language, one that came much later in the course of history. Class I was obviously the latest, for it had only thirty-two signs and was of an alphabetic type—that is, each letter represented a sound.

With this important distinction made, scholars went to work on the writings of the first class. The great Persian kings were in power from the sixth century to the middle of the third century B.C. If the ancient writers who made the inscriptions had any sense of diplomacy, the first column of writing must have been in Old Persian, the language of that era. Since something was already known of this dead language, the groundwork was laid for the first breakthrough in translation.

While all this linguistic wrangling was going on among recognized scholars in the cultural capitals of Europe, an obscure language student in Germany was working on his own translation of the Class I symbols. Georg Grotefend was a teacher of Greek at a small *gymnasium* (high school) in Göttingen. He had neither the time nor the money to make journeys to Persepolis to copy inscriptions or to engage in lengthy arguments over the correct meaning of a certain wedge-shaped mark in a tablet of clay. He had friends among these argumentative scholars, however, who sent him copies of the Persepolis inscriptions.

In 1802 Grotefend began a careful study of the writings and, noting that some signs occurred with greater frequency than others, made the logical deduction that they must be vowels. Since the tombs and columns had been erected to honor the Persian kings, it seemed reasonable that the names of these kings must figure largely in the inscriptions. Rulers such as Darius and Xerxes were not noted for modesty. Their sculptured memorials showed them with their arrogant heads held high, often with one foot implanted on the neck of an unfortunate foe. Obviously any written record must refer frequently to such men by name.

Grotefend then chose the places where the names Darius or Xerxes and such probable words and phrases as *king* and *son of* fitted into the vowel pattern. He managed to make a rough reading, adding other letters as the inscription began to make sense. When he sent his translation to his friends, they accorded him only a grudging admiration for his brilliant work. He was by no means a member of the inner circle of scholars who had made the study of cuneiform their particular concern. Although he set forth some claims that were later proved to be incorrect, he was the first to find the key to the Class I inscriptions at Persepolis. He did this some thirty years before the remarkable and romantic Henry Rawlinson appeared on the scene.

Rawlinson knew nothing of Grotefend's work when he first came to Persia. But using the same system of inspired guesswork, manipulating vowels and known names, he made a translation of a short inscription at a place called Mount Alvand. Later, he worked on the Persepolis inscriptions and succeeded, as Grotefend had done, in deciphering some of the names and phrases relating to the great Persian dynasty.

The writings at Mount Alvand and Persepolis were too short, however, to give him the vocabulary he needed. So, in 1835, he turned his attention to the massive Behistun Rock, which Darius I had erected in the fifth century B.C. Here on the 1,200 square feet of sunbaked surface were hundreds of lines of trilingual script written in columns. The Old Persian alone contained more than 400 lines of text. The Class II and Class III inscriptions were shorter. Rawlinson set out to copy all three classes. In two years of grueling labor, often in temperatures as high as 120 degrees Fahrenheit and with the help of his active young Kurd assistant, he was able to get down no more than 200 lines of the Old Persian.

At night he worked on his translations in a little hut made of palm leaves and cooled by a continuous stream of water poured over the roof by his faithful helpers. In this damp shelter he managed to decipher some of the hundreds of place names the text contained.

Rawlinson made a tremendous impression on the Persians of his day, which may explain why they were so ready to help him in his work. Tall, vigorous, and dynamic, he caught the Persian imagination and earned their ungrudging esteem. One elderly Turkish official who worked for Rawlinson during this period tells that Rawlinson

lived here for twelve years, and each year his power became stronger. And toward the end of his time, had he taken one dog and put his English hat on his head and sent the dog [to the bazaar], all the people would have made way for him

and bowed to him.   And the soldiers would have stood still
and presented arms to him as he passed.   . . . in knowledge
and learning [Rawlinson] was like a god; as a horseman, he
was like Antar [an ancient Arabian warrior]; as a king, he
was like Nimrod, and when he spoke at the town council
of Baghdad the heart of the Pasha [ruler] melted and the
knees of the councilors gave way under them.

It was even said that on one occasion Rawlinson knocked together the heads of two Pashas who were quarreling and holding
up business.   A man of such talents and courage deserved to
be a hero.

The Class II inscriptions inspired even more violent disputes
among the scholars than the Old Persian.   This syllabic lan-

But Rawlinson was an officer in the army on leave from active
service.   During these years his military duties called him
away.   It wasn't until nine years later, in 1844, that he was
able to return to the Behistun Rock to finish copying and translating the Class I columns.   Now that the Old Persian could
be deciphered, Rawlinson and other scholars were ready to go
to work on the other two classes.   By 1850 Rawlinson had left
the army and had himself transferred to Baghdad, where he
served as British Consul General.   In this post he was relatively
free to devote himself to what was to become his lifework,
the study and deciphering of ancient languages.

The Class II inscriptions inspired even more violent disputes
among the scholars than the Old Persian.   This syllabic language was given several different names in the course of the
arguments.   Today, however, it is called Elamite.   The Elamites were a people who lived in what is now western Iran,
with Susa as their capital.   They had used some form of cuneiform writing since 2600 B.C.   But the form of writing common
to the Elamites in the sixth and seventh centuries, when the
Behistun Rock inscriptions were made, was that used for Class

These symbols at the left illustrate the progression from a simple
pictograph through varying stages to sophisticated cuneiform script.

II.   The same sign in the Elamite inscriptions often had a number of meanings, and it is easy to understand why Rawlinson and his friends battled so long over their translations. But with the knowledge that each of the three classes on the great Behistun Rock was the same inscription, they at least had a foundation on which to work.

The crisis in this literary conflict came in 1857. Rawlinson and four other famed language scholars were invited to send translations of a chosen inscription to the Royal Asiatic Society in London. All the translations were sealed, to be opened only by a committee of experts from the Society. The scholars accepted the challenge. When the envelopes were opened, the committee found that the translations were so nearly alike that linguistic scholars all over the world were convinced that Rawlinson and his friends were on the right track. The science of Assyriology was really born with that contest. The heat of battle over the cuneiform translations was allowed to cool and the study of these ancient languages went on in relative peace.

Class III presented fewer difficulties than the previous classes, for scholars had a tremendous amount of material, aside from the inscriptions on the Behistun Rock, with which to work. Since the bricks and tablets found at Babylon were inscribed with the Class III form of writing, this language was called Babylonian; it was the language used during the period of the Babylonian empire, from Hammurabi's day on through the reigns of the great kings Nebuchadnezzar, Sennacherib, and Ashurbanipal.

All during the time of these early cuneiform studies it was assumed that the Babylonians were responsible for the invention of cuneiform writing. This was chiefly because so many of those old bricks and tablets were found in the ruins of Babylon. But as these Babylonian inscriptions were translated, it soon

The symbols on the right are part of a cuneiform inscription.

became apparent that many of the old bricks and tablets used words that were not of a Semitic origin. The names that occurred in many of the inscriptions were quite unlike those of the familiar Babylonian kings. Now scholars were convinced that these names must refer to a people who had lived long before the great days of the Babylonian empire. Therefore, they reasoned, cuneiform writing must have been used by a people who lived and wrote long before the Babylonians pressed their history into clay.

Rawlinson, who by this time was back in England, had come to much the same conclusion. The vocabulary just wasn't right for the Babylonians. But it was a French scholar, Jules Oppert, who won the distinction of tracing these first writings to the Sumerians.

In 1869, Oppert delivered a lecture in Paris in which he stated that these early people should be called Sumerians, because the title King of Sumer appeared so often on these old tablets. His use of the name was confirmed when the ancient Sumerian city of Lagash was uncovered near the modern city of Telloh in the 1870s. The statues and bas-reliefs found there showed a people much different in feature from the Babylonians, and clay tablets revealed a political and religious history that had begun much earlier.

After thousands of years of dusty death, Sumer was at last on the map. The tablets unearthed at Lagash were chiefly inventory lists, records of commercial transactions, and legal documents. But they revealed a great deal about the life of these very practical Sumerians. The clay documents also gave the names of thousands of people, places, and gods. Later on at Nippur, diggers uncovered a vast library of literary works and, even more valuable to modern scholars, grammars and dictionaries. The discoveries were proof that as long ago as 3000 B.C. a written language had existed in Sumer. The illustration shows the development of cuneiform writing.

As we know, the people of the Uruk period first used pictorial

Early Pictographs	Archaic Cuneiform Signs	Objects
		Plow
		Sledge
		Boat (with Sails?)
		Chisel
		Ax
		War Mace

Examples of pictographs and cuneiform characters.

writing as long ago as 3500 B.C. These earliest pictographs were scratched on stone, as the illustration shows, and represented a simple picture of a foot, a man, or a house. Since stone was so scarce in this sandy area, even the earliest Sumerian writers began to use common clay for their writing tablets. A handful of this "river mud" was molded into a rough rectangular form, about four by six inches in size. The reeds along the marshy banks were cut slantwise to form a crude stylus and so the distinctive shape of cuneiform writing was established.

The earliest picture writing used curves and straight lines, but it was difficult to make these on damp clay. The wedge-shaped stylus was too stiff and could only follow such lines or

51

curves with an approximation of their shape. A close study of the progress of writing shows how the reed stylus first followed the ancient picture writing, then gradually developed a "shorthand" of its own. We do not know exactly when the reed stylus was first used or when the various modifications were made, but the writing naturally grew more sophisticated over the centuries. By 2300 B.C. it was being used throughout the Middle East.

Germans, French, English and Americans have contributed enormously to the understanding of this ancient civilization. The Russian scholar Igor Mikhailovich Diakanoff's work has done a great deal to bring the Sumerians vividly alive in the modern world. In America, the most noted Sumerologist is Samuel Noah Kramer.

Samuel Noah Kramer was born in Russia and came to this country as a child. A graduate of the University of Pennsylvania, he studied under an eminent professor of Assyriology who stirred his imagination and guided him to his lifework. The enthusiasm he brings to his studies blows like a fresh wind over this dusty field of learning. He has written a definitive history, *The Sumerians,* and a fascinating smaller work, *History Begins at Sumer,* in which he sets forth "Twenty-seven 'Firsts' in Man's Recorded History."

Our knowledge of the history of the long-dead Sumerians is still growing as scholars continue to translate the wedge-shaped markings on the old clay tablets. The Sumerians are by no means dead. They are coming to life on these bits of baked clay where writing first began.

The cylinder seal at the left makes the impression shown at the right. British Museum.

chapter 4

A STRANGER IN NIPPUR

LONG, long ago, in the time of Sumer's Golden Age, a man traveled northward from his home, Erech, to Nippur on a secret mission for his king. The Sumerian city-states were in constant rivalry with one another; Erech at this time was jealous of Nippur's power and prestige as a cultural center. The stranger covered by boat the seventy-odd miles that lay between the two cities, following for hours the curving course of the wide Euphrates as it rolled through the fertile plain. The boat was a long, narrow vessel, high fore and aft, and was rowed by a dozen oarsmen seated amidships in pairs.

The riverbanks were wide bands of green, dotted with date palms and thick patches of reeds. Near the half dozen cities that lay between Erech and Nippur the belts of green broadened out into cultivated fields and pasture land, vineyards and groves of fig trees. These lands were the property of each walled city. Their size and state of cultivation were an indication of the city's prosperity.

The river itself was a lively place, for the muddy waters of the Euphrates provided the broad highway between one Sumerian city and another. Many of the craft were long trading vessels, such as the one in which the man from Erech journeyed. Among them were vessels capable of traveling long distances. Sometimes, aided by a huge square-shaped sail, they ventured far out on the wide waters of the Mediterranean Sea to the west to bring cedars from Lebanon or stone and precious metals from the lands to the north. Smaller basketlike boats were more common. They crowded the waters, particularly near the wharves of each walled city.

The traveler, seated in the stern in the shade of a brightly colored awning, was a square, solid man with dark hair parted in the center and hanging in a thick mass to his shoulders. His face was clean-shaven; his large nose and heavy-lidded eyes were typical of most Sumerians—the nobility, the merchants, and the workers who tilled the fields along the river. But unlike the workers in their short and sensible tunics, this man wore an elaborately flounced skirt and a fringed shawl draped over one shoulder, leaving the other bare. These garments showed that he was a man of consequence, perhaps a member of the nobility, an impression to which his bearing as well as his clothing contributed. He sat upright. His prominent eyes took in everything along the riverbanks and on the water.

In the fields and vineyards surrounding the walled cities which he passed, workers were gathering in the harvest. The grain and grapes were placed in huge baskets and tied on either side of donkeys, the ever-present beasts of burden. Often they passed a man carrying a laden basket on his back. Both men and beasts were taking the harvest to the temple compound within the city. There it would be allotted and distributed to the people. Most of the goats, sheep, and cattle grazing in the pastures outside the city walls belonged to the temple, which was the soul and center of every Sumerian city.

The complicated networks of canals that kept these fields and pastures green were the responsibility of a special group of workers; their job was to tend the canals that let water into each field, making sure they were free of silt, opening and closing the interlocking waterways as need arose. These canals were like a vast arterial system through which flowed the lifeblood of each city.

The stranger's boat was approaching Nippur. The high walls of Sumer's cultural city rose splendidly above the broad fields that stretched away for miles on either side of the river. As the stranger looked up at these towering ramparts, he remembered the words of the hymn that celebrated this great city of nearly 200,000 people. Nippur was "fearsome and awesome" in its grandeur. The rising tiers of the great temple did much to make it so. This was Enlil's temple, "the Ekur, the lapis-lazuli house, the lofty dwelling-place."

According to Sumerian belief, each city belonged to the god who had been placed in charge of it when the world began. Sumer's highest deity was Enlil, the air god. In fact, as the stranger knew, the word Nippur meant "the place of Enlil." Thus, Enlil owned Nippur and the words of the same hymn

This map, by far the oldest in the world, was dug from the ruins of Nippur in 1899 by an expedition from the University of Pennsylvania.

Originally found in a terra-cotta jar, the map became part of a private collection belonging to Hermann Hilprecht, the leader of the expedition and an eminent professor of Assyriology at the University. During his lifetime very little was done to interpret the old map, though it was published as a blurred photograph in one of Hilprecht's books. After his death in 1925, his entire collection of cuneiform tablets was bequeathed to the University of Jena in Germany. Professor Kramer was granted permission to study the Hilprecht Collection in 1955, and he is the scholar responsible for the interpretation of this view of ancient Nippur.

The map was drawn about 1500 B.C., long after the "stranger" about whom you will read in this chapter made his journey to Nippur. But a city, even though it was destroyed by conquerors like the Gutians or the Babylonians, was rebuilt very much as it was before. The temple particularly was always reconstructed on the same sacred site. Therefore, it is fairly safe to assume that the Nippur of 1500 B.C. was little different from the city which the hero of the story visited on his mysterious mission in Sumer's Golden Age, around 2100 B.C.

stated that "only to his exalted vizier [the priest] . . . did he make known . . . his orders." Enlil was capable of taking terrible revenge on those who defiled his temple. When Sargon's son sacked Nippur, some three centuries earlier, Enlil, "like the Bull of Heaven," had crushed the enemies "who dared assault the Ekur."

Although the temple and its high priest owned most of the land surrounding the city, the stranger knew that a good share belonged to the *ensi*, the governor who ruled by the will of his peers. At one time this leader had been elected by the people to take power only in times of crisis, such as war between the city-states or the threat of foreign enemies.

But over the years the ensi, a man chosen for his military

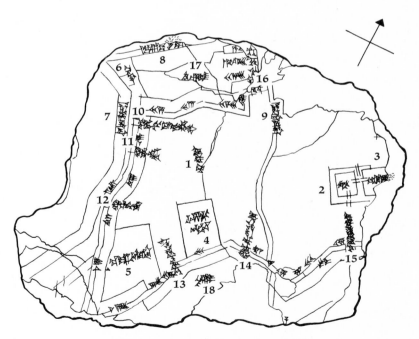

Map of City of Nippur about 1500 B.C.

prowess, had assumed greater power and, with the army behind him, had established himself as hereditary king. Now in this Golden Age, he was the leader responsible for his city's prestige in war and peace. The palace rivaled the temple in magnificence and in the breadth of its lands outside the city walls.

Sumer was a communal democracy where the common man had a chance to better himself by his skill and industry. Nearly everyone—the farmers, fishermen, tradesmen, and craftsmen who made up the greater part of Nippur's population —owned a plot of arable land, even though it might be only a few feet in area. Each man could hope for the time when his personal god might be good to him and raise him higher on the social and economic scale. A free market allowed him to buy and sell, and many a noble had his beginnings in a more humble way of life. The stranger did not have to be told these things, for it was the same in Erech.

The traffic thickened as the long, high-decked boat drew nearer to Nippur. Along the city wall that bordered the river, wharves reached out into the water. Beside each wharf clustered trading vessels, fishing boats, and flat barges heaped with grain. The men at the oars of the stranger's boat had to pause in midstream, to await their turn to dock.

The river curved inward toward the city, touching the walls near the lower gate. Here it swung westward, leaving a broad strip of cultivated land between the water and the southern walls of Nippur. As the rowers feathered their oars, the stranger took a piece of baked clay from beneath his cloak. It lay flat on his hand, this small tablet measuring about 7 by $8\frac{1}{2}$ inches. On it was a carefully drawn map of Nippur. In the shelter of the folds of his cloak, he studied the markings on the hard clay. Why the stranger needed the map with its indication of the principal buildings, the placement of the city gates and waterways was his secret. He had no intention of sharing it with the men of Nippur. How he came by this map and who had drawn it for him was his secret also.

The stranger made note of the position of the city gates and considered his chances of entering with the least risk of being discovered. The Great Gate (No. 12 on the map) was obviously the largest and, since most of the trading vessels were collected at its docks, the most closely guarded. Off to the right, across the fields, were three other gates. The nearest was the Nanna Gate (No. 13). Nanna was god of the moon, whom the stranger hoped might be kind to him. He gave a sudden order to the oarsmen, signaling them to pull in to the less crowded wharf below the city walls.

Before slipping the map beneath his cloak, the stranger once more checked the position of the other gates beyond the Nanna Gate. The first was the Erech Gate (No. 14). In the distance was the Ur Gate (No. 15), and just below the Ekur (No. 2) with the most sacred temple the Kiur (No. 3) behind it. The position of these gates told the stranger that the mapmaker had done his work well, for he had tipped his map at a 45 degree angle to make these gates face southeast in the direction of Erech and Ur. A moat (No. 18) ran parallel to the southern wall. But the dock toward which his boat was headed lay inside this stretch of water and the stranger did not have to cross a bridge to reach the Nanna Gate.

The long boat tied up to the wharf at last amid shouts and cheerful cursing. The stranger made his slow, dignified way along the crowded dock, being careful to avoid attracting attention to himself. But his keen eyes missed nothing. The logs of cedar heaped along the wharf told him that Nippur was trading with the northern provinces, where the trees grew in the great forest of the mountains. The bars of gold and copper were evidence that Nippur was in touch with the lands to the east. He took careful note of these signs of prosperity. Later, he would hire a scribe to write his observations with a stylus on a soft bit of clay. He himself could not write; that was an art for the learned men and was perhaps beneath his dignity as a member of his king's household.

Once beyond the dock area, the stranger followed a hard-packed dirt roadway leading toward the Nanna Gate. Here, between the moat and the city wall, was a maze of flat-roofed mud-brick houses. It was as though these hovels, clustered against the protecting walls, were trying to push their way into the city. The farmers who dwelt here were responsible for the fields and vineyards beyond the moat and had to live within sight of them.

The stranger had no wish to lose himself in the tangle of narrow alleys that ran among these houses, so he kept to the main highway. It broadened out as he came nearer the gate. Like the wharf area, it swarmed with activity. A cloud of dust rose above the laden donkeys; herds of sheep and goats were being pushed and prodded along in the direction of the gate. Wheeled carts, heaped with goods and produce, rattled past, drawn by oxen or by pairs of donkeys. The crowd grew thicker as the massive gate loomed closer.

A shouted order sent the entire throng scurrying back. A two-wheeled military chariot drawn by four donkeys swept out from the city. A driver, wearing a bronze helmet, stood on the axle, supporting himself by gripping a fleece-covered head-board. He guided the donkeys with long leather reins fixed

"The Stranger in Nippur" travelled in a long boat similar to this Assyrian naval vessel. British Museum.

A wealthy Sumerian lady of the court wears a stole.
Louvre.

to their noses by a ring. After the chariot, marching four
abreast and wearing leather tunics, came a detachment of foot
soldiers. Their highly polished short swords and shields
gleamed in the sun. This was a guard detail, one of the many
who watched over the city. The stranger, from his place in
the shadow of the gate, observed that the soldiers looked tough
and hardy, a fact that would interest his king.

Now that he was about to enter the city itself, the stranger
mingled with a group of men dressed much as he was. They

were merchants or temple administrators whom he had seen on his way toward the gate, and he joined them unobtrusively. No one took special note of him, although he was on the alert as he went past the guard. Now that he was within the city, he could move about freely. He lost no time in making his way toward the higher ground to the east.

But first he passed through the labyrinth of narrow streets lined with mud-brick houses very like those outside the wall. The area did not show on his map, but it was here that the workers lived. Fat, brown children played naked in the dust, adding their shrill voices to the shouts and curses of the street. Many of the houses contained shops. The clang of metal from a forge, the rasp of a saw from a woodworker's shed, or the whine of a potter's wheel added to the general noisy confusion.

The crowded one-story houses presented a blank wall to the street, except for their low doorways and tiny windows near the flat roof. Behind that wall a family might live in crowded discomfort. But this house was the owner's castle, where each family member had rights and privileges.

Occasionally the stranger caught a glimpse of the life within and was struck by the light and color that seemed to bounce off the dull mud walls. The women's long, loose-fitting garments, caught at one shoulder and hanging to their feet, were of bright hues—green, yellow, or scarlet. The bedding mats, hanging over the edge of the roofs to air in the sun, were a blaze of color.

The family slept on the roof these warm nights, and stairways led up to this open area along the outer walls. Later, in the cold months, they would huddle in one of the tiny rooms, wrapped in shawls and woolen blankets. A fire in an open brazier would help ward off the night cold. The smell of dried dung, often the only fuel, wouldn't bother them, for they were used to it. However, anyone with a sensitive nose suffered on the streets or in the houses of a Sumerian city. There was little

Sumerian chairs appear modern as well as beautiful. British Museum.

concern for sanitation; the air in these narrow streets was thick with every imaginable human and animal smell.

But the stranger was accustomed to the noise and the hurly-burly of crowded streets; it was the same in his own city. Nevertheless, he made mental notes of the activity, for the health and attitude of these lowly classes interested him. A happy and contented citizenry was vastly important to a city's well-being. It was one sign of a well-organized and prosperous community.

Remembering the map he carried, he pushed his way through the knots of people, keeping his eyes on the tiered tower of Enlil's temple to the east. A little farther along, in a more open area near the Nanna Gate, the stranger came to a wide patch of green, the park in the center of the city (No. 5). Here were trees, shrubs, and flowers growing beside paved walkways. Massive pieces of sculpture stood among the greenery. Those statues probably represented the gods and kings of Nippur; but

63

his own city had similar sculpture, and the stranger had no time to waste on a pleasant stroll.

In this prosperous section, he was more concerned with examining the imposing houses that lined the wide streets. Here, where wealthy citizens lived, the way of life was vastly different from that in the workers' quarters. The houses were built of mud bricks to be sure, but the bricks were whitewashed and imbedded with brightly colored stones and tiles set in rich mosaic patterns. The windows in the high outer walls were larger and had bars made from the same mud bricks. In each house, a wide doorway opened into an entrance hall. Another showed an open courtyard beyond. This was the heart of the house.

(Below.) Gold Objects found at Ur, a bowl and jewelry, reflect the high level of craftmanship in cities such as Nippur. University Museum of Philadelphia.
(Opposite.) This gold cup belonged to Queen Shubad. When found it contained some of the Queen's green eye paint. British Museum.

The stranger walked more slowly now, often pausing to gaze into courtyards.   These were large, light-flooded areas, many of them encircled by a two-story balcony from which hung woven tapestries.   The inner walls were also whitewashed and provided a quiet backdrop to the brilliant colors of the hangings.   Behind the columns surrounding the court was a shadowed walking space where statuary was set in niches in the wall.   Large glazed pottery jars caught and reflected the light from the sunlit open space.

The rooms opening out from this inner court were hidden from the stranger, but knowing the houses of his own city, he had an idea what they were like.   One room was set aside as the household shrine, dedicated to the worship of the personal god who watched over the daily life of the master of the house and his family.   Prayers and offerings were made every day to this god.   As a result, the god was expected to take special care of the worshippers.   The entrance hall, which the stranger could see dimly in the light from the courtyard, was furnished with highbacked settees and chairs, and the floor was covered with bright reed matting.   This was the place where a guest such as he might be received by the master of the house and his wife, if he were bidden to dine.   But the stranger was an observer in Nippur, not a guest, and he was careful not to make his presence known.

This charming domestic scene was found on the walls of the palace at Ninevah, about 700 BC. Museum Barraco of Rome.

The dinner hour was approaching; slaves were setting out the evening meal on low tables in the inner court. Huge plates made of copper or decorated pottery appeared, heaped with pomegranates, dates, and figs. Bread in vast round loaves and baked fish were the principal dishes. Earthen vessels foaming with goat's milk and beer made from barley were set about on the tables. Some of these containers were made of gold; they were graceful, fluted cups or bowls, sometimes with a spout. But the gold ware was less common than copper dishes or clay pottery. The stranger realized that the former was displayed only on some great occasion. In such houses he saw musicians tuning their lyres and harps.   The guests were to be entertained with song and poetry recitals during the feast to come.

As these wealthy citizens gathered, the stranger had a chance to study them.   In one house the women were emerging from the upper rooms that led off from the second-floor balconies. They wore brilliantly colored flounced garments reaching to their ankles, the upper part elaborately folded over their shoulders, leaving their necks bare to display necklaces and long, dangling earrings.   The ornaments were often made from colored stones or shells; only the very wealthy could afford lapis lazuli, carnelians, and gold.   But the jewelry was intricately designed to set off the women's dark hair and skin to advantage.   Their large eyes were blackened with malachite, which they had applied before bronze mirrors in the privacy of their own quarters.

The men, even these prosperous citizens, were dressed much like the stranger, although their garments were of richer material and were more elaborate in color and design.   Many of them were as clean-shaven as he was.   Others, however, wore beards, combed and carefully curled, and so long they fell down over their bare chests.   Perhaps they had no fancy for the copper razors the men of Sumer sometimes used.

The slaves who did all the menial work in these houses interested the stranger particularly.   Their number was an indication of Nippur's prosperity.   Such evidence was of special concern to his king at Erech.   The slaves—men, women, and children brought back in chains from a conquered city—were regarded as among the most important spoils of war.   Bought and sold in the marketplace, they belonged completely to their masters.   If a slave tried to escape, he was beaten, then branded as an example to others who might harbor similar hopes.   A healthy slave was more valuable, however, and such mistreatment was meted out only to the most unruly spirits.

Some of these slaves, as the stranger very well knew, were citizens of Nippur who had broken the law.   A man in debt

This head of a man was fashioned about 3000 BC.   Chicago, Oriental
Institute, Museum of the University.

often had to sell himself or members of his family for a specified number of years in order to pay off his obligations. Sometimes his children were offered as such a sacrifice. But he did have a second chance. Sumerian society was always practical, and certainly wanted no revolt on its hands from desperate slaves. A slave could therefore earn his freedom by working in his spare time. These earnings were his own and with them he might buy his way to freedom. He thus contributed to the general economy as well.

The stranger was now approaching the center of the city. He paused a moment in the shadow of a building which was marked on his map as the Anniginna (No. 4). It was a huge, mysterious enclosure with high walls and no windows, built close against the city walls between the Nanna and Erech Gates. Throughout all Sumer, Nippur was famed as the city with the most complete archives. Perhaps the Anniginna was where the archives were kept, but the stranger doubted this. These valuable legal, commercial, and literary records, inscribed on tablets of clay, were more likely to be stored in a building within the temple compound. In any case he was wise enough not to display unseemly interest in this high-walled structure. It might attract attention to himself, and as long as he had the map in his possession he must remain unnoticed.

There were other places in which it would be unwise to show too great an interest. One was the Lofty Shrine (No. 6) on the upper left-hand corner of the map, a sanctuary built where the Euphrates (No. 7) joined the Great Wall (No. 17). Beyond was the Canal (No. 8) where the god Enlil first saw his future wife at her bath and fell in love with her. This myth was as familiar to the stranger as it was to the people of Nippur. If he were to inspect such distant places, it meant he would have to risk passing through another of the three gates in this area of the city. The Nergal Gate (No. 16) was named in honor of the god of the lower world; the stranger had no wish to incur his suspicion. The Gate of the Sexually Impure (No. 10) did

not concern him, and the Lofty Gate (No. 11) was too far from
the only place of any real interest, the Lofty Shrine. But this
temple was doubtlessly well guarded and accessible only to its
priests.

Now that he was well within the city, he dared not jeopardize
his mission by showing unnecessary curiosity. He passed an
inn a little beyond the Anniginna, a comfortable-looking place
with a pleasant tree-shaded courtyard. Dinner was being set
out for wayfarers such as he. The stranger took note of it,
deciding to return later to seek a meal and room for the night.
But first he wished to take advantage of the remaining daylight
to see all that he could of the city.

Another area he was careful to avoid was one not marked
on his map at all. That was the king's palace. A high wall
surrounded the grounds and buildings in the center of the city,
and the gate to the royal compound was well guarded. But
the stranger was familiar with the palace at Erech and had every
reason to believe that Nippur's king lived in the same luxury
and grandeur. Where the wealthy had fine houses and dozens
of slaves, the king had several such houses. He also had a
veritable army of servitors to wait upon him, his queen, and
his harem. Since chance visitors were not looked upon with
favor in the king's domain, the stranger kept well away from
its entrances.

The *Shatt-en-Nil* (No. 9), the Midcity Canal, cut through
the center of the mapped area. The man from Erech crossed
it in company with a pack of laden donkeys whose drivers were
herding them toward the temple compound on the high ground
to the east. The bridge was a steeply arched structure rising
high above the muddy water that flowed between the stonework
sides of the canal.*

The stranger had no hesitation in making his way toward

---

*The measurement of this canal is proof of the accuracy of the ancient map. Its
width is given as 4 *gar* (a gar was about 20 feet) and the dried-out course of the
Shatt-en-Nil in the ruins of Nippur is just 80 feet wide.

The funeral stele of a priest was decorated with this dining scene. Louvre.

the gate that cut through the outer wall of the temple enclosure. Here was the heart of the city's life and the citizens of Nippur were free to come and go within its confines. But the temple itself was another matter; the stranger dared not encroach upon such sacred precincts. Only the priests of the god Enlil were admitted to those tiered towers.

But there was plenty to observe and study within the outer compound, a vast area that was like a city itself. Although craftsmen and artisans worked in their own shops, as the stranger had noted, here were more shops to accommodate the variety of workmen who labored for the temple. These community craftsmen worked in a special section set apart for them. Tanners made harnesses, armor, and leather tunics for the soldiers and even containers for storing food. Carpenters sawed and hammered out a wide variety of objects—some as small as a spindle for a loom, others as large as a cart for the drovers. The pottery shops whirred with activity, for clay was

71

the raw material most widely used in nearly every phase of Sumerian life.

Herds of sheep and goats were kept penned in the compound, until their wool could be sheared, washed, and carded before being sent to the weavers. Most of the weaving was done by women slaves on large, flat looms. Woolen cloth was a valuable item of commerce, often traded with other countries for metals. The stranger, therefore, was especially careful to observe the size of the herds and the number of weaver's shops.

Each shop and industry inside the temple grounds was supervised by an administrator appointed by the priestly hierarchy. These officials were everywhere. They were called clients and were an important factor in the Sumerian order of society. They kept account of each day's work—the number of bowls made in a potter's shop, the progress of a piece of sculpture for the inner sanctuary. Of the four classes, the nobility, ordinary citizens or commoners, clients, and slaves, the clients were the ones who did the most to make the system work. Dependent on the temple or palace, they administered the complicated machinery of temporal and religious life. The scribes who recorded the progress of the craftsmen, the size of the fishermen's catch, and the products of field and pasture were also classed as clients, for their carefully kept accounts were the basis of the system.

Other administrative clients were responsible for making proper allotments of raw materials to qualified recipients. A certain amount of barley, for instance, went to the brewery. So much was earmarked for the bakers, so much as feed for the cattle. In each craft and industry these allotments were calculated so that every man and beast might have his share.

The archives building, although unmarked on the map, was close to the temple walls. The stranger could distinguish it by the surge of activity near its entrance. Here the records of city transactions were kept; an army of scribes worked within these walls. Even more important was the vast library that was

Nippur's greatest claim to fame. As the cultural center of Sumer, the city had seen to it that the library contained copies of all the myths, legends, and literature of the land. Other cities kept records and made literary collections. But the ones at Nippur were the most complete. The stranger knew that his king would be interested in a report of the contents of the archives building. He joined a group of administrators and scribes who were making their way toward the huge building.

Already dusk had fallen over the city. The stranger hoped that in the push and hurry of the moment he might pass into the building unnoticed. Keeping well within the center of the group, he was hustled through the entrance into the dimly lighted interior. The administrators and scribes scattered in different directions and the stranger was left conspicuously alone in the vast inner court. Some light filtered down from the open area above him, showing a network of rooms in the two stories above the colonnaded court. Obviously the records were stored here, with a special room for each category.

But the light also showed the stranger a guard, moving purposefully toward him from the shadows beneath the colonnade. He had no wish to be found with the map in his possession, for it was the one thing that could betray his mission. A terracotta jar stood near him in the open court and the stranger moved quickly to stand beside it. Pretending to settle his cloak about his shoulders, he let the incriminating map fall from his hand into the wide-mouthed jar. He heard it drop with a clink and turned to face the guard.*

The stranger was fated never to see that map again. Though he was not detained, and returned safely to Erech to make his report to his king, the map lay hidden in the pottery jar for nearly 3,500 years.

---

*Exactly how the map got into the terra-cotta jar is a mystery and probably will remain so. The foregoing story, however, is the author's imagined version.

The statue of the ruler of **Mari**, about 3000 BC. Museum of Aleppo.

chapter 5

THE SUMERIAN SCHOOLBOY

WHERE did you go?

In the ancient Sumerian city of Erech a ten-year-old school-boy stood uneasily before his father in the family reception room. The older man, seated in his highbacked chair, made a majestic figure in his draped cloak with its heavy fringe. He was a scribe in the temple courts. Because of his writing skills he was a man of importance in the city.

How could the boy tell his father that he had not been at school that day, because he had gone to see the great river in the full flood of spring?

I did not go anywhere.*

That morning before dawn he had left his bed on the flat roof where all the family slept in warm weather. School began with the rising of the sun. The boy had taken the rolls his mother gave him and left the house at the usual time.

In the half-light of morning there was a freshness in the air.

---

*Nearly four thousand years after this fatherly questioning was pressed into a damp clay tablet in cuneiform script by a Sumerian scribe, a book was published in the United States called, *Where Did You Go? Out. What Did You Do? Nothing.*

Instead of the steady, dusty wind of winter, he caught the damp scent of the river beyond the city walls.   He had watched the Euphrates in flood in other years.   It was exciting to see how the river swelled and rose above its banks, rising even to the tops of the date palms along its edge; to see how it flowed out over the adjacent flatlands, leaving a thick layer of mud to enrich the wheat and barley crops.

The schoolhouse, the *edubba,* was connected to the temple and stood within the shadow of its walls.   The way to it led along a narrow, twisting street.   The tower of the temple rose high above the brick-and-mud walls of the houses that lined the street before him.   Presently the boy turned aside down a narrow alley to a gate in the city wall.   Beyond the gate were the open fields and the wide flowing waters of the river.

> If you did not go anywhere, why do you idle about?   Go to school, stand before your School Father, recite your assignment, write in your tablet. . . .

The father was thundering now.   He adjured his son to "be a man," not to "wander about in the public square," and accused him of wasting "day and night in pleasure."

A Sumerian schoolboy of 2000 B.C. could scarcely be blamed for playing truant.   He started school when he was a small child and stayed there until he was a young man and a graduate scribe.   The school day began at sunrise and lasted until the sun set.   Discipline was immediate and harsh; the cane was punishment for sloppy work, for inattention or the slightest infringement of the rules.   Even the big brothers, the monitors who assisted the head teacher, were free with the stick.

The schoolhouse itself was something less than a cheerful place.   Lighted by small, high windows, it was airless, hot in summer and chillingly cold in winter.   A tablet, excavated not many years ago from the ruins of Ur, presents a vivid picture of the activity and argument within the confining walls of a

Sumerian school. A monitor addresses an unruly student in the following terms:

> Why do you behave like this? Why do you push, curse and hurl insults . . . ? Why do you raise commotion in school? . . . Why were you insolent? . . . If I did to you what I pleased . . . I would beat you . . . put copper chains on your feet . . . lock you up in the [school] house. . . .

With such a prospect before him, even the most hostile student might think twice before he pushed, cursed, or hurled insults. On an average day, the Sumerian schoolboy studied the tablet he had labored over the day before. His assignment might be to copy an ancient myth or epic, the usual form of exercise in the long process of learning to form the cuneiform signs neatly and correctly. When the tablet had dried, he could only review his mistakes: he could not correct them.

Thousands of these practice tablets, some of them marked in very shaky script and obviously the work of the very youngest students, have been dug from the ruins of early Sumerian cities. Other texts are written so well that they must have been done by an older student or even the *ummia*, the "expert" who was the school father.

Past errors reviewed, the boy was given a fresh tablet for a new effort. These were made for him by a big brother, who took a blob of wet clay and pressed it between his hands into a thick flat tablet about nine inches square. Then, while it was still damp, the boy began his day's task.

The practice tablets found in the rubble are almost uniform copies of literary compositions. Some of them are no more than fifty lines, others a thousand. Many of them repeat the myths and epics dealing with the mighty deeds of the Sumerian gods. There are hymns to these deities, too, and essays retelling proverbs and fables.

A later record, composed about 2000 B.C., gives an account of a typical school day.

. . . When I awoke early in the morning, I faced my mother and said to her: Give me my lunch, I want to go to school. My mother gave me two rolls and . . . I went to school.

The ummia, who seems to have composed this document as an exhortation to other struggling students, then goes on with a dialogue between master and pupil that was clearly meant to illustrate a model situation.

What did you do in school?
I recited my tablet, ate my lunch, prepared my [new] tablet, wrote it, finished it; then they assigned me my oral work, and in the afternoon they assigned me my written work. When school was dismissed, I went home, entered the house and found my father sitting there. I told my father of my written work, then recited my tablet to him, and my father was delighted.

If the boy's reply reflected a lack of enthusiasm for the day's activities, his attitude seems to have been accepted by his contemporaries as a normal one. Twenty-one copies of this essay, some of them fairly well-preserved, others in fragments, have been found in the ruins of Sumerian tablet houses, as the schools were called.

The finding and piecing together of this particular record and its eventual translation is an adventure story in itself. The middle part of one tablet was discovered and translated in 1909. But in its broken form, it made little sense. Over the next twenty-five years many scholars worked on various bits and pieces. But in 1938 Samuel Noah Kramer, the Sumerologist who has done a major part of the modern work on these remarkable documents, found a four-column tablet that contained a copy of the main body of the text. By piecing together fragments from museums as far apart as Philadelphia and Istanbul, he was able to construct a complete document which he could study. The final translation was published in 1949,

Clay "envelopes" contained letters and documents of commercial transactions. About 2000 BC. Postal Museum, Paris.

forty years after the first tablet was discovered and nearly four thousand years after it was impressed on clay.

The Sumerians were the first people in the history of the world to make use of a system of writing. Thousands of small clay tablets, inscribed in the early pictograph writing of about 3000 B.C., have been uncovered in the old city of Erech. These are chiefly economic documents, noting trade transactions and business deals. But some are word lists and were probably meant to be used by students for vocabulary study.

By 2500 B.C. the cuneiform method was developed by the Sumerians and writing became a formal school study. In the next ten centuries the schools became increasingly professional as the training ground for the army of scribes who kept the records of Sumer's economic, cultural, and religious life. During this period the scholars, scientists, and mathematicians of ancient Sumer collected their wisdom within the mud-brick walls of the edubbas on thousands upon thousands of baked-clay tablets.

Not every boy had the opportunity to study this art. Only the rich and well-born were sent to school, many of the students being the sons of scribes. Scribes held high places in the Sumerian social and economic order; there were thousands of them, each trained for a specific purpose. Some were royal scribes. These acted as the king's secretaries, transcribing his orders, writing histories of his deeds and exploits, or extolling his virtues as a ruler.   Others were temple scribes who performed the same service for the all-powerful priests.

With such prospects in view for his son, it is hardly surprising that the same father who scolded his boy for wasting his time felt that the youth was missing a golden opportunity.   The father himself was a scribe, proud of his craft and the rewards it brought him.

> Among all mankind's craftsmen, . . . no work is as difficult as the scribal art.   It is in accordance with the fate decreed by Enlil that a son follow the work of his father.

In order to make the importance of his craft even clearer and at the same time point out the difference between his lot and that of other, less fortunate boys, the father describes the life the sons of the poor and uneducated must lead.

> I, never in my life did I make you carry reeds to the canebrake.   The reed rushes which the young and the little carry, you, never in your life did you carry them.   I never said to you, Follow my caravans.   I never sent you to work to plow my field.   I never sent you to work to dig up my field. . . .   Go, work and support me, I never in my life said to you.

The father knew very well what he was talking about when he urged his son to achieve success.   Training as a scribe was the gateway to opportunity.   Tablets dating from about 2000 B.C. list hundreds of scribes and describe their fathers' occupations. These men, who had begun their careers as scribes, were now ambassadors, city fathers, temple administrators, sea captains, or officers in the army.   Others held important posts as tax officials, accountants, or foremen.   Some even became priests, whose authority as representatives and interpreters of the will of the gods was supreme.

A son who did not follow in his father's footsteps had no

hope of becoming a leader in his community or one of its important citizens. Girls had no such choices; none are listed among these scribes. Although they probably didn't "carry reeds to the canebrake" or plow a field, they were confined to the house to work with their mothers and to learn the housekeeping arts.

The schools were originally established as training grounds for administrative posts in the palaces and temples. This was to be their principal purpose throughout their existence, but they gradually assumed a wider function as centers of culture. In the materialistic Sumerian scheme of things, schools were the only institutions with any concern for preserving or developing scholarship.

The curriculum widened to include sciences, such as mathematics, biology, and astrology, and the more practical studies such as farming and economics. Textbooks were compiled in each of these fields and became the standards for all the Sumerian schools. They reveal a knowledge of natural science that is remarkable for its time. Lists of trees, birds, and insects were compiled; stones and other minerals were enumerated in their proper classifications; the known countries and cities were listed. Mathematical problems and tables were worked out and preserved on clay tablets. A study of the Sumerian language with its complicated linguistic forms was an important part of the school curriculum.

After Sumer was invaded by the Akkadians under Sargon I, the Sumerian scholars realized a need for a dictionary of their language. The Akkadians themselves, having no written history, borrowed one from the Sumerians, along with their scribal art and their literature. The dictionaries the Sumerian scribes wrote used both Sumerian and Akkadian words. In this way they preserved in script the language of Sumer. Centuries later, when Sumer was conquered by Hammurabi of Babylon, Sumerian was forgotten as a spoken language.

Although a schoolboy spent most of his time copying and

Sumerian tablets usually dealt with practical matters. This one
demonstrates math problems. British Museum.

recopying these texts and had no thought of doing any creative
writing, some of the teaching scribes did original research and
writing. The professor who composed the popular sermon on
the schoolboy's ideal day was just such an originator. Often

a school father devoted his life to teaching, with no thought
of going on to one of the better-paid administrative posts in
the temple or palace. He depended for his wages on the tuition
fees paid by his students and could never look forward to being
as important or wealthy as most of his graduates.

But the scholar-scientist of the Sumerian schools lived longer
in history than any of his contemporaries. By inscribing on
clay the myths, hymns, tales, and accounts of his time, he has
left for us all that we now know of ancient Sumer. The same
scribe who urged his son to follow the work of his father ends
his plea with a blessing that sheds light on his hopes for future
glory:

> May you be the head of your city's sages,
> May your city utter your name in favored places,
> May your god call you by a good name.

This worshipper, with his
head held high, was
found near Erech. British
Museum.

chapter **6**

GREAT GODS OF SUMER

"And the Lord God caused a deep sleep to fall upon Adam . . . and He took one of his ribs . . . and . . . made . . . a woman."

The biblical account of the creation of the first man and first woman in the Garden of Eden is familiar to everyone. But the Book of Genesis, where the story of Adam and Eve occurs, was written in the ninth century B.C. Two thousand years before that the Sumerians inscribed on clay a myth which may have inspired the Bible story.

According to Sumerian belief there were four all-powerful creating gods in the universe: An, Enlil, Enki, and Ninhursag.

The "exalted lady," who "nourished" the Sumerian rules, was Ninhursag, the mother of all living things. She occupied herself in the creation of man and in bringing green things to earth. The garden she brought to life in Dilmun, the paradise of the gods, may well have been the original of the Garden of Eden. Here in the "land of the living" she made green plants flourish, and from here the waters of the world flowed. The Sumerians believed that this garden of the gods existed somewhere to the east. It was a "pure land," fresh and bright, that knew neither sickness nor death.

86

Terracotta bas relief showing a musician with lyre.
Louvre.

Ninhursag created eight special plants for Dilmun. But her
brother, Enki, unwisely ate them one by one. Instantly eight
of his bodily organs weakened and he wasted almost unto
death. As the myth relates, "Thereupon Ninhursag cursed the
name of Enki: 'Until he is dead I shall not look upon him with
the eye of life.'"

Idi-Narum, known as "the miller," lived in Mari.
Museum of Aleppo.

But Enki was not without persuasive powers and he at last got Ninhursag to help him. She proceeded to cure his eight ailing organs by creating a special god to heal each one. When she came to Enki's ribs, the poem says:

> My brother, what hurts you?
> My rib hurts me.
> To the goddess Ninti I have given birth for you
>   [answered Ninhursag].

It was Ninti's job to cure Enki's rib and she did her work well, for Enki continued to flourish in the pantheon of the gods throughout Sumerian history. Ninti's name means "lady of the rib" as well as "lady who makes live." In biblical literature the Hebrew name Eve also means "she who makes live." If both Ninti and Eve had one meaning in common, then it is not difficult to imagine why the Hebrew scholars gave Eve Ninti's other characteristic and created her from Adam's rib.

The Sumerians looked upon the universe as a huge, hollow mountain whose base was the flat disk of earth and whose top was the high arc of heaven. The lord of heaven was An and his lady was the Earth.

At one time, An was supreme in the pantheon of the gods. His seat of power was Erech, where a temple was dedicated to his worship. But after 2500 B.C., An began to slip into the background, perhaps because his son, the air god Enlil, took such an active part in worldly affairs. Nippur was Enlil's city, and his temple, the Ekur, the high holy place of Sumer.

The earliest cuneiform records describe Enlil as "the king of heaven and earth" and "the father of the gods." Perhaps the Sumerians had a right to look upon Enlil as "the king of

Few painted frescoes such as this one from Mari, have been found in the cities of Sumer. A sacrifice appears to be taking place. Louvre.

all the lands," for it was he who "made the day come forth" and who felt compassion for man in his pitiable weaknesses as well as his triumphs.

Enlil concerned himself with matters great and small. He planned the moon and stars, the pickax and the plow. The closing lines of a Sumerian hymn pay tribute to his powers and performance:

Without Enlil, the great mountain,
No cities would be built, no settlements founded,
No stalls would be built, no sheepfolds established,
No king would be raised, no high priest born . . .
Workers would have neither controller nor supervisor . . .
The rivers—their floodwaters would not overflow,
The fish of the sea would lay no eggs in the canebrake,
The birds of heaven would not build nests on the
    wide earth,
In heaven the drifting clouds would not yield their
    moisture,
Plants and herbs, the glory of the plain, would fail
    to grow. . . .

Inanna, goddess of love, was worshipped in this stone temple at Erech.

The great Enki was the most active of the gods. He was the water god and the god of wisdom, who "knew the very heart of the gods." The nether world, the *abzu*, was his dwelling place and his temple was at Eridu. Enki carried out Enlil's commands and did the actual work of creating, after Enlil had formed the master plan. The Sumerian writers and philosophers had no scientific approach to nature or the study of the origins of life as we know it. "Enki did it" was their answer to all questions of creation.

"Enki and the World Order" describes what Enki himself thought of his marvelous feats.

> My father the king of heaven and earth . . .
> Gathered all the divine laws, placed them in my hand . . .
> I, the lord, firm is my command, I lead it forth,
> At my command stalls are built, sheepfolds are enclosed;
> I approach heaven, the rain pours down from above,
> I approach the earth, there is a mighty inundation. . . .

After Enki had done the heavy work of "budgeting the accounts of the universe," he was ready to "go forth in his land" and set about his duties of earthly creation. With no false modesty, he takes credit to himself for creating the rivers and for filling them with fishes, for the winds and the "thundering storms." Then:

> The plow and the yoke he directed,
> The great prince Enki . . .
> Opened the holy furrows,
> Made grain grow in the perennial field . . .
> Grain he heaped up for the granary . . .
> He multiplied abundance for the people. . . .

But the four creating gods could not do the work of the world alone and they brought into being an enormous array of lesser gods. The moon god, who was known as Sin or Nanna, was

Enlil's son and he in turn was the father of the sun god, Utu, and Inanna, the goddess of love. After An declined in prestige, Erech became Inanna's city. Utu, the sun god, went on to create the rest of the heavenly bodies: the planets, "the big ones who walk about like wild oxen," and the stars, "the little ones who are scattered about like grain." These gods of the heavens had more power than some of the more mundane gods like Kabta, who was god of the brickmold, or Nibaba, who had control of the measuring rod.

Great or small, each of the gods was responsible for some phase of Sumerian life. They were extremely active in carrying out their various duties and seeing to it that the other gods didn't usurp their powers or jockey them out of place in the heavenly hierarchy.

Dilmun, the "mountain of heaven and earth, the place where the sun rose," and the home of the gods, was as lively and filled with strife as any human abode. For the Sumerians considered the gods' behavior as human as their own, even though they were immortal. These heavenly beings had passions, hates, loves, and desires. They ate and drank, they married and had families. When they had to go about their business in the world, they traveled as best they might; the moon god by boat and the sun god in a chariot. The storm god was more fortunate, for he could ride the clouds.

The higher gods had establishments in Dilmun, but they also were thought to inhabit the special temples dedicated to them. How Enlil, for instance, could be in Dilmun and in his temple at Nippur at the same time was a problem that never troubled Sumerian worshippers. He was a god and could obviously perform wonders. But in his earthly home, the sacred inner sanctum of the temple, he required food and drink. It was the duty of the high priest to provide for him. The wood or stone statues, which represented the god in each temple, were fed every day with the very best the city had to offer. How the god managed to dispose of his food and drink must have created

The goddess Bau was greatly revered in Lagash and
associated with ceremonies dedicated to Ningirsu.
Museum of Baghdad.

a housekeeping problem that only the high priest and his assist-
ants knew how to cope with. The average Sumerian was only
required to believe that his city's god was well nourished.

The gods, generally, operated in a spirit of good will. They
lived by the *mes*, the divine laws that governed the universe.
An ancient Sumerian document lists more than a hundred of

93

these mes which had to do with all aspects of life, both on earth and in the realms of the gods. Enki had charge of these divine rules and it was part of his duty to see that they were obeyed so that the universe could operate in an orderly way.

Man himself, according to Sumerian belief, was a poor creature, "fashioned of clay" and with but one purpose in life—to serve the gods. In fact, before Enlil broke the earth with his pickax and men began sprouting up like plants, the gods had rather a thin time of it. They implored Enlil to give them slaves from among the newly born men, so that they might be relieved of their humdrum work. As a later god, Marduk of the Babylonians, expressed it, "Let him [man] be burdened with the toil of the gods that they may freely breathe."

Completely enslaved by the immortals, man had no control over his own destiny. Neither was there any way for him to know what the capricious gods had in mind for him. His sense of helpless dependence is shown in the lines of a poem:

Mere man—his days are numbered . . .
Whatever he may do, he is but wind.

A portion of one temple uncovered near Erech. About 2000 BC. State Museum of Berlin.

Beset by the uncertainty of his god-controlled life, a poor mortal had nothing to look forward to either. When he died, his spirit descended into the abzu, that dark and dismal nether world, "the land of no return," where Enki dwelt. Here he could spend eternity contemplating his wretchedness, for death was his lot and only the gods were immortal. The Sumerians never questioned this bleak arrangement; the gods had planned the universe in this way and man must obey the divine order.

But this dreary concept was made bearable by the hope that the gods really preferred goodness and truth to falsehood and injustice, and would reward those qualities. More than 4,000 years ago the rulers of Sumer boasted that they had been chosen by the gods to bring "law and order to the land." (When we hear this ambition being expressed by leaders of today it casts an interesting reflection on man's progress through the centuries.) Utu, the sun god, was in charge of the moral order, but his handmaiden was Nanshe, who played a more active role in seeing that justice was done to mankind. A hymn found at Nippur describes some of her duties:

To comfort the orphan, to make disappear the widow.
To set up a place of destruction for the mighty,
To turn over the mighty to the weak . . .
Nanshe searches the heart of the people.

The fact that the gods included evils in their divine mes shows the Sumerian's realistic view of the world order. "Never has a sinless child been born to his mother," said one of their poets. Realizing his helpless state, mere man had only one recourse—to appeal to his personal god. This special god acted as an intermediary between man and the higher gods. The latter were considered to be much too busy to heed a single mortal's prayers.

A man's good angel, however, was nearer the heavenly throne. Therefore, he had a chance of getting the attention of the really powerful gods in times of stress.   In order to impress his personal god with the importance of his sufferings, a man could never blame the gods for his misfortunes, for they were entirely without fault.   If he had any hope of salvation, it was up to him to bow before his personal god and wail over his shortcomings.

Even though each man had his personal god, the compelling force in his life was the high god who inhabited the temple in each Sumerian city.   Enlil was in fact the real ruler in Nippur, as Enki was lord of Eridu.   The temple was the soul and center of the city.   Within these temples the high priests interpreted the will of Enlil or Enki—or whichever god dwelt in a city's temple—and only through these priests were the divine orders carried out.   In Enlil's case, for instance, a hymn exalts the relationship between priest and god:

> Only to his exalted vizier . . .
> Did he commission to execute his all-embracing orders,
> Did he entrust all the holy rules, all the holy laws.

Even the kings of each city-state were no more than temporary tenants of the god who owned it.   "Since the god rules, all citizens were equal in his service.   Sumerian society was cooperative, with every detail carefully planned.   In Sumerian documents the workers on the temple estates, priests, herdsmen, fishermen, gardeners, etc., were referred to as 'people of the god X.'"*   In spite of this concept of equality in the eyes of the god, it must often have occurred to some of the toilers in the fields that the high priests and great kings were more "equal" than they.

With every phase of life regulated by the god whose statue was thought to be his actual presence within the temple, the Sumerians spent a great deal of time in ceremonies and festi-

---

*Leonard Cottrell, *The Quest for Sumer.*

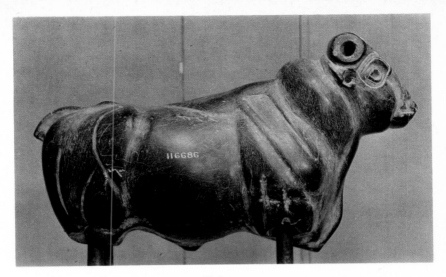

The black bull figured prominently in religious ceremonies such as the one which preceeded the covering of the kettledrum. British Museum.

vals which would appease or flatter this mighty force in their lives.

The life of all was regulated by a calendar which harmonized society's progress through the year with the succession of the seasons. A recurring sequence of religious festivals interrupted all business and routine at frequent intervals; several days in each month were set aside for the celebration . . . of the moon in one of its phases, and other natural occurrences. The greatest annual event in each city, which might last as long as twelve days, was the New Year's festival, celebrated (in the spring) at the critical point of the farmer's year when nature's vitality was at a low ebb and everything depended on the turn of the tide. . . .*

These ritual acts were very elaborate and were carried out in a way that made a mystery and ceremony of every detail of temple life. As an example, an ancient document gives a careful set of complicated rules which were to be followed "when covering the Temple Kettledrum."

*Henri Frankfort, *Birth of Civilization in the Near East.*

. . . An expert shall inspect—from head to tip of tail—a sound black bull whose horns and hooves are whole. If its body is black as pitch, it shall be taken for the ceremony. If it is spotted . . . or if it has been struck with a staff . . . it shall not be taken for the ceremony. . . . On the bull you shall perform the rite of Washing the Mouth. You shall whisper through a reed tube into the bull's left ear the incantation . . . You shall purify the bull, using a brazier and a torch. . . . Then you shall cut open that bull and start a fire with cedar. You shall burn the bull's heart . . . remove the tendon of the left shoulder and shall bury the body of the bull wrapped in a single reed . . . [and] arrange it so that its face points to the west. . . .*

After so much time and careful effort on the part of the temple authorities, it's a wonder they ever got around to covering that kettledrum with the beleaguered bull's much-purified hide.

But for all their fear of the god who ruled their lives from his inner sanctum in the temple, the Sumerians must have felt that this mighty deity cared for them. A hymn to Enlil extols not only his powers, but the benefits he brought to his people in Nippur:

> Enlil, whose command is far-reaching, whose word is
>   holy . . .
> The unrighteous, the evil, the oppressor . . .
> The arrogant, the agreement-violator,
> He does not tolerate their evil in the city . . .
> Enlil's house is a mountain of plenty . . .
> Its loftiness reaches heaven's heart. . . .

And from this mountain of plenty the Sumerians looked for their salvation on earth, though heaven's heart was beyond their expectations.

---

*James B. Pritchard, *Ancient Near Eastern Texts.*

chapter 7

THE WORKING WORLD OF SUMER

In days of yore a farmer gave these instructions to his son: When you are about to cultivate your field, take care to open the irrigation works so the water does not rise too high in it.

MORE than 3,600 years ago Ninurta, the "trustworthy farmer of Enlil" and the god of the South Wind, began the first Farmers' Almanac with these words of sound advice. Though Ninurta was Enlil's son and one of the mighty gods of Sumer, evidently he felt he couldn't speak directly to the people, even on such an important subject as farming. So he wrote his almanac as though he were a farmer giving advice to his son. Since neither Ninurta nor any farmer was educated in scribal arts, the real author of this document was undoubtedly a teacher in an early Sumerian school. Meant to serve as a guide to successful farming, this manual proved so popular that it was copied and recopied many times. Bits and pieces of its clay tablets have been uncovered in many digs throughout the land that was Sumer.

Agriculture was the backbone of Sumerian life. It was one of the reasons the black-headed people had been able to develop a culture in the Land between the Rivers, and was their mainstay throughout their history.

Behind their success as farmers was an even more astonishing skill as engineers. A complicated network of canals and irrigation ditches watered the arid desert, a tremendous engineering feat even by modern standards.   This irrigation system forced each community to live and work together, for the canals had to be maintained for the good of all.   Even one stopped-up ditch might endanger the working of the entire system.   At one time in Sumer's history, as an ancient myth relates, a terrible drought occurred.   The gods who were in charge of irrigating the fields were in despair, for even the Tigris was without "good" water.

> Famine was severe, nothing was produced,
> At the small rivers, there was no "washing of the hands,"
> The waters rose not high,
> The fields are not watered.
> There was no digging of irrigation ditches,
> In all the lands there was no vegetation,
> Only weeds grew.
> Thereupon the lord put his lofty mind to it,
> Ninurta, the son of Enlil, brought many good things into
>   being.

Once Ninurta had put his lofty mind to it, he called down the waters of heaven and directed them into the Tigris, which was now able to flood the fields in the usual way.   And the myth goes on to say:

> Behold now, everything on earth,
> Rejoiced afar at Ninurta, the king of the land.
> The fields produced abundant grain . . .
> He made happy the spirit of the gods.

With powerful Ninurta to guide him, the Sumerian farmer had good reason to follow the mighty god's advice, as passed on through the good offices of the schoolman scribe.   His instructions were detailed, including such matters as seeing that the farmer "watch the field's wet ground . . . let no wandering ox trample it.   Chase the prowlers and have it treated as settled land."

Even the tools were not to be neglected. "Let your tools hum with activity. . . . Your new whip should be fastened with nails and the handle to which your old whip was fastened should be mended by the workers' children."

But the plowing and planting were most important, for as Ninurta said, "sustenance is in a plow." The Sumerian plow was a seeder as well as an earth turner. A cylinder seal found at Nippur shows a picture of this dual instrument, which not only dug a furrow, but planted seed "uniformly three fingers deep."

Once the seed was in and the "sprout has broken through . . . shoo away the flying birds . . . water the top seed." Then on through the growing season with its various waterings, until the farmer is admonished to "harvest the grain at the moment of its full strength." Here the gleaners must be watched so they "do not tear apart the sheaves." They must also leave enough of the fallen grain on the ground for the needy to gather and thus grant the farmer "everlasting favor" with the gods. All this was encompassed in "the instructions of Ninurta," whose "praise is good."

The Sumerians raised not only wheat, millet, and barley, the most important grains, but a variety of vegetables as well. Peas, onions, lettuce, and turnips were staples of their diet. Indeed, the rich river valleys, inundated each spring by the Tigris and Euphrates, were the garden of the ancient world.

The farmer's skill and his success in following Ninurta's

directions gave him a high place in Sumerian economic life for another important reason.   Sumer lacked such natural minerals as building stones and precious metals.   Nor were there any trees, except for the date palm, which was cultivated for its fruit but whose wood was too soft to be used as building material. With their abundance of grain, however, the Sumerians had a product worth trading.   Their long boats, some of them as large as five tons' capacity, sailed the Mediterranean coasts and ventured as far as India and Ethiopia.   From these distant lands the trading vessels returned with the gold and precious metals of the Indies and the wood of the Ethiopian forests.

The larger seagoing boats probably used sails as well as oars: a model of such a sailing boat was found in the ruins of Eridu. But the more common river boat was round like a basket and made of woven reeds, covered with animal skins.   These boats were drawn along the riverbanks by men or beasts, or rowed. The Sumerians referred to them as "the turnips."   Large or small, the turnips crowded the waterways of Sumer.

On land, goods were moved by sledge or by carts pulled by oxen.   These beasts were ideal for heavy work because they could be trained to harness and were strong enough for such tasks as pulling loads of stone.   Donkeys were used for war chariots and the lighter wheeled wagons.

Woolen cloth was another article the Sumerians used widely in trade with foreign countries.   The textile industry was probably the greatest commercial enterprise of the Land between

(Opposite.) Models of boat used in Sumer about 4000 BC. National Museum of Science and Technology. Milan. (Right.) Wooden wheel found at Ur was made about 2500 BC.

the Rivers, for the herds of sheep and goats were prized nearly
as much as grains and produce.   Thousands of tons of wool
were grown each year in a single city-state.   The process that
converted the raw wool into cloth was watched over by the
temple administrators in every detail.   The sheep and goats
were "sheared" by plucking, the wool spun on hand spindles
by female slaves.   The weaving itself was done on flat or
horizontal looms by teams of three, who might spend several
days preparing a piece of wool cloth some three or four yards
square.   The cloth was soaked in a large vat containing an
alkaline solution by a person called a fuller.   He then tramped
over it with his bare feet.   At that point the wool was ready
to be stretched, dried, and used as an article of trade.   Although
some flax was raised, the linen cloth was reserved for the high
priests, who were evidently entitled to wear something finer
than wool.

The importance of the farmer and the shepherd in Sumerian
life is illustrated by a lovely poem.   In it the sun god, Utu,
tries to persuade his sister, Inanna, the goddess of love, to marry
the shepherd, Dumuzi, rather than the farmer, Enkimdu.   The
very fact that so high a lady would consider marrying either
of these workingmen is proof of their standing in Sumerian
society.

> Oh, my sister, let the shepherd marry you . . .
> His cream is good, his milk is good
> . . . everything his hand touches is bright.

But Inanna is stubborn and decides on the farmer:

> Me the shepherd shall not marry . . .
> His fine wool shall not cover me,
> Me, the maid, the farmer shall marry . . .
> The farmer who makes grain grow abundantly.

Dumuzi had persuasive powers, however, and he outlined his
advantages over the farmer:

The farmer . . . what has he more than I . . .
Enkimdu, the man of dike, ditch and plow . . . ?
Should he pour me his prime beer,
I would pour him, the farmer, my yellow milk for it . . .
Should he give me his good bread,
I would give him, the farmer, my honey-cheese for it . . .
After I shall have eaten, shall have drunk,
I would leave for him the extra cream. . . .

No doubt persuaded by such evidence of generosity, Inanna consents to marry the shepherd, Dumuzi. Fortunately, Enkimdu accepts his defeat without rancor.

I against you, shepherd . . .
Why should I strive?
Let your sheep eat the grass of the riverbank,
In my cultivated lands let your sheep walk about. . . .

The poem ends as the rejected farmer offers a wedding gift: "I will bring you wheat, I will bring you beans. . . ." As it turned out, Enkimdu had rather the best of the bargain. In-anna proved to be a hot-tempered lady who at one point

Grain was cut with sickles such as this one from Ur. British Museum.

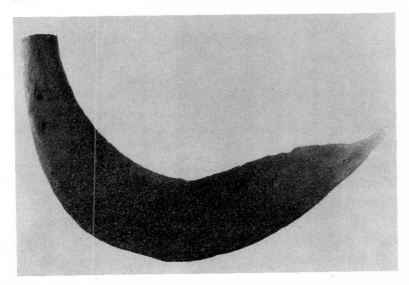

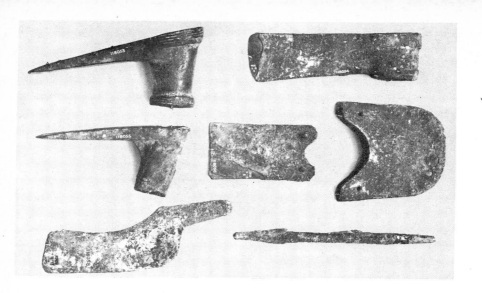

This assortment of frequently used bronze weapons includes an axe, pick, knife and harpoon. British Museum.

consigned poor Dumuzi to the nether world, where he languished for some time before she relented and set him free.

Perhaps the poem was meant to serve as a lesson to its readers in a sensible way to end a quarrel, but it also illustrates the necessary amity in which the Sumerian farmer and shepherd lived. As the leading producers of the time, they had to sink or swim together.

The Sumerians are credited with a number of inventions, all of them proof of their practicality and ingenuity. Since clay was the only available natural mineral, they put it to use as a building material and invented the brick mold to insure uniform bricks. The wagon wheel and the potter's wheel were first used by the Sumerians, as the ancient bas-reliefs show. They did casting in bronze and copper, both imported materials. In architecture the Sumerians were the first to use the arch, vault, and dome. Everything they invented helped to move mankind forward on the long road toward civilization.

The craftsmen who labored at the potter's wheel or hammered out a plow or a wheel may not have had the social standing to think in terms of marrying a goddess, but they were

important in the Sumerian economy. Their products, dug from
old ruins, tell almost as much about this ancient way of life
as the cuneiform tablets. Even though Sumer lacked wood,
stone, and metal, these craftsmen were highly skilled in their
arts. Many of them had come from distant lands to practice
their trade in Sumer. Sir Leonard Woolley found a tablet at
Ur which lists the amount of work done during a single year
in the city about 1975 B.C. Eight workshops are mentioned:
the "houses" of the chisel worker or sculptor, the jeweler, the
lapidary, the carpenter, the smith, the leatherworker, the fuller,
and the basketmaker.

The sculptors and jewelers will be discussed in another
chapter. The other craftsmen, working in more mundane materials, created the goods the Sumerians used in everyday life.

The fuller, as we know, was the man who tramped on the
woven wool to make it soft, and he seems to have had only
a small shop, for he is given little space on the old tablet. But
the metalworkers, who got their gold, silver, tin, lead, copper,
and bronze from foreign lands, were kept busy from dawn to
dusk. It was their job to make the copper or bronze hoes, axes,
chisels, and knives, as well as saws, nails, and even the copper
mirrors for the highborn ladies. Instruments of war were a
metalworker's responsibility, too. The lance points, swords,
and daggers all came from his shop. Copperwork was highly
developed; the fires that heated the metals were made from reed
bundles. A foot-operated bellows kept the fire at the proper
heat for melting copper.

A carpenter was hard put to find wood; the imported hard-
woods—oak, fir, and ebony—were far too costly and often the
carpenter had to use the wood from old objects to fashion new
ones. Sir Leonard's tablet tells how three tabletops and four
fir boxes were recut to make one table, two beds, and a small
box. Boat-building and chariot-making were also the carpenter's responsibility, and the new wood was doubtless saved for
these more important articles of war and commerce.

As for the basketmaker, his work was relatively simple, though widely useful on all levels of society. With the abundance of reeds along the riverbanks, he had materials at hand for the baskets the farmer used to carry his produce, the smaller baskets of the housewife, and even the turnip boats.

The skins the leatherworker had at his disposal were as various as the animals the Sumerians raised or killed in the hunt. Bulls, calves, goats, pigs, and sheep were common domestic animals; antelope, wild asses, and boars were hunted in the open country. Their skins were used for everything from harnesses and saddles to shoes and waterbags. The leather was tanned with such alkalies as sumac. Sometimes it was decorated with "powder of gold," probably for the goods of the nobility and the harnesses of the military chariots. Leather reins were used on the war vehicles. The soldiers wore leather tunics; they carried leather shields to intercept the spears and arrows of their foes as they marched to battle in four-column formation.

With so many uses for leather it is no wonder the Sumerians took good care of their beasts and paid such particular attention to animal husbandry. Their food supply depended to a large degree on the sheep, pigs, and cattle they tended. They relied on donkeys and oxen for transportation. Some two hundred Sumerian words meaning "sheep" have been translated, indicating the importance of this all-purpose animal in Sumerian life. Just as the fishermen and fowlers caught the fish of the rivers and the birds of the air, any living creature that was worth eating or whose skin might be useful was shot by bow and arrow, netted, trapped, or hooked by the Sumerians.

It was perhaps because of this key role animals played in their lives that the Sumerians created so many animal fables, preceding those of Aesop by some thousand years. The dog, which seems to have been looked upon as a nuisance by these practical people, is the subject of more than eighty proverbs or fables. Cattle, donkeys, and the fox or wolf follow next in order of

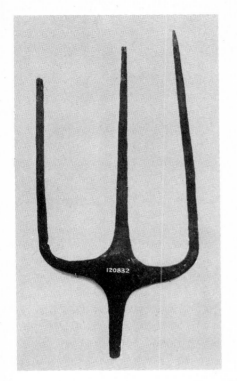

(Left.) Bronze trident from Ur was used for spearing fish.
(Right.) Vessels for carrying liquids were often made of animal gut.
British Museum.

popularity, with the monkey coming in for a lesser share of attention. These tales, as with Aesop's, are meant to point a moral, using animals to illustrate a human sin or error.

Packs of wild dogs roamed the countryside. For this reason, they were looked upon with fear and dismay as the following proverb shows: "The ox plows, the dog despoils the furrows." Or "It is a dog that does not know its home."

An early Sumerian who "counted his chickens before they were hatched" had his folly illustrated by another proverb involving the elusive fox: "He did not yet catch the fox, yet he is making a neckstock [yoke] for it."

In the following brief fable the wolf shared honors with the fox as a crafty and deceitful animal:

109

Nine wolves and a tenth slaughtered some sheep. The tenth one was greedy and . . . said, "I will divide them for you! There are nine of you, and so one sheep shall be your joint share. Therefore, I being one, shall take nine. This shall be my share."

How the greedy wolf hoped to convince his friends that this was a fair distribution of the spoils the proverb doesn't reveal. But another saying about the fox gives a good idea of the low esteem in which he was held: "The fox gnashes his teeth, but its head is trembling."

The mongoose was kept as a pet in Sumer to chase the rats and mice, but the little animal seems to have been as gluttonous as he was useful. "If there is any food around, the mongoose consumes it," says a proverb with a sort of despair.

The elephant, which must have been a rare beast in Sumer, was put in its place by a small bird, the wren.

The elephant boasted about himself, saying, "There is nothing like me in existence! Do not [compare yourself to me]." The wren answered him, saying, "But I, too, in my own small way, was created just as you were."

The earliest reference to horseback riding was found on a tablet in Nippur and indicates that the horse was used as a domestic animal as early as 2000 B.C. The slight fable reads, "The horse, after he had thrown off his rider, said, 'If my burden is always to be this, I shall become weak.'"

As for the monkey, his position in the animal hierarchy is clearly illustrated by the following: "All of Eridu is prosperous, but the monkey of the Great Music Hall sits in the garbage heap." Obviously the monkey was looked upon as a source of entertainment even in those early days. A later scribe mocked the poor creature even further when he wrote a letter from a monkey to its mother:

To Lusalusa, my mother . . . thus says Mr. Monkey: "Ur is the delightful city of the god Nanna, Eridu is the prosperous city of the god Enki; but here I am, sitting behind the doors of the Great Music Hall. I must eat garbage; may I not die from it! I don't even get a taste of bread; I don't even get a taste of beer. Send me a special courier—Urgent! "

In spite of the importance of crafts and commerce to their welfare, the Sumerians knew that, in the final analysis, it was agriculture that formed the real basis of their economy. A literary "debate," a favorite form of Sumerian composition, involves two gods, Enten and Emesh, each of whom claims to be more important than the other. They fall into a quarrel and decide to appeal to the great god Enlil. Enten has the first word:

Father Enlil, you have given me charge of the canals,
   I brought the water of abundance,
Farm I made touch farm, heaped high the granaries,
I made grain increase in the furrows . . .
Now Emesh . . . has no understanding of the fields,
Has jostled my . . . arm and . . . shoulder. . . .

Unfortunately Emesh's answer is unintelligible on the old tablet, and even his jostling, which shows the argument must have grown rather warm, seems to have been ineffective. Enlil gives his verdict thus:

The life-producing waters of all the lands—Enten is
   in charge of them,
Farmer of the gods—he produces everything,
Emesh, my son, how do you compare yourself with your
   brother Enten!
The exalted word of Enlil . . . who dares transgress it . . .
Enten, the faithful farmer of the gods . . . proved himself
   victor . . . Father Enlil, praise!

The code of Hammurabi, the great law giver, appears on this huge
stele. Louvre.

chapter **8**

LAW IN SUMER

DURING the reign of Ur-Ninurta a barber, a gardener, and an unnamed man murdered a temple official at Isin. The name of the unfortunate victim was Lu-Inanna. But what this strange trio had against him was not mentioned on the old tablet which tells the tale. Even stranger, it was this trio who informed the murdered man's wife, Nin-dada, that her husband, Lu-Inanna, had been killed. Nin-dada was brought into court to testify. Apparently, being a woman of strong good sense, she "opened not her mouth, her lips remained sealed."

But Nin-dada's silence proved to be no protection for the killers. Moreover, it put her own life in jeopardy, for there were courts of law in the land of Sumer. The king ordered the three men and the silent wife brought to trial at the Citizen's Assembly in Nippur, the capital city just to the north of Isin.

In the Assembly, nine men led the prosecution. "They who have killed a man are not worthy of life. Those three males and that woman should be killed in front of the chair of Lu-Inanna. . . ."

But two assemblymen objected to including Nin-dada in the indictment. As it turned out, Lu-Inanna, the victim, had been remiss in providing support for his household, and her defender argued, "A woman whose husband did not support her, after she heard that her husband had been killed, why should she not remain silent? Is it she who killed her husband? The punishment of those who actually killed should suffice."

The justice of this opinion carried weight with the Assembly and the three men "were handed over to the executioner to be killed," while Nin-dada went free.

This ancient murder trial suggests that, although the kings of the various Sumerian city-states had vast powers, they were not allowed to rule as military dictators or tyrants. The judges saw that the laws were obeyed. Each city-state had its representative assembly, freely elected by the people. These congresses consisted of an upper house, or senate, composed of important citizens, and a lower house, made up of men who could bear arms. Thus, five thousand years ago the Sumerians took a long step toward democratic government. As far as the historians know, they were the first people in the world to elect representatives to decide the important issues of the day.

We will see later on that even the great hero Gilgamesh had to appear before "the convened assembly of the elders of his city" before he undertook one of his warlike adventures.

But to the average Sumerian, the law codes, instigated by some of the more enlightened rulers, were even more important than the influence of an elected assembly. They assured each citizen that he had a democratic right to his day in court.

"The Case of the Silent Wife" must have created something of a stir in Sumer, for it was recorded on several clay tablets. Thousands of other legal documents dug from the old cities give evidence of a highly developed system of laws and codes, the first legal regulations in man's history. Until recently it had been supposed that Hammurabi's famous code, inscribed on a huge stele about 1750 B.C., was the oldest body of laws in the world. But excavators in the sands of Sumer have unearthed codes far older.

The need for reform is as old as history itself.   When people left their isolated farms and villages to live together in crowded cities, man's inhumanity to man took its natural course: the rich oppressed the poor, the strong bullied the weak.   About 2350 B.C. in the city of Lagash things had come to such a state that the people rose in rebellion and chose a new ruler.   This man,

Urukagina, "established the freedom" of the city by instituting a set of reforms. So far as we know, these are the first laws designed to safeguard the rights of the ordinary citizen.

The laws themselves show only too clearly what the people of Lagash had to put up with in their daily lives. A contemporary who made one of the several copies of the ancient laws described what was happening in Lagash nearly 4,500 years ago:

> Formerly ... the boatmen seized the boats. The head shepherd seized the donkeys. ... The man in charge of the fisheries seized the fisheries. ... The oxen of the gods plowed the onion patches of the *ensi* [ruler] and ... the cucumber fields of the ensi were located in the god's best field.

(Left.) "The Silent Wife" probably dressed as did this woman of Mari. Museum of Damascus. (Right.) Sumerian official stands in the position of worship, a favorite of artists and their patrons. Louvre.

It is not difficult to read between the lines of this complaint; obviously there was war between the temple and the palace and, for the moment at least, the king had the upper hand. He was making use of the "oxen of the gods" to plow his own onion patches and had appropriated the god's [temple's] best fields.

The condition of the poor was lamentable, as the document goes on to relate: the "artisans had to beg for their bread. The apprentices had to take the food leavings at the great gate [of the palace]." And, even worse, from one end of the land to the other "there was the tax collector." In those days the rulers of Lagash wrung the last penny from their subjects and from the cradle to the grave forced them to pay taxes to the palace. In time "the houses of the palace . . . and the fields of the palace . . . crowded each other from side to side;" even the priests could do nothing against the heavy power of the temporal rulers.

But the oppressed citizens knew when they had had enough. Once the corrupt dynasty was overthrown, the new ruler,

Sumerian men were usually bearded. This bust shows one who was cleanshaven. Louvre.

Urukagina, proved to be their savior. Urukagina acted as representative for the god Ningirsu, who had evidently been as completely cowed by the former ruler as the people themselves. But Urukagina was a god-fearing man and obviously a person with a strong sense of justice. The documents give an account of his social reforms. Here the word *freedom,* as related to mankind, appears for the first time in all history. That word was *amargi,* which literally translated means "return to the mother." But amargi had a more positive significance in the laws Urukagina put into effect.

Now the boatmen, the owners of cattle, and the fishermen were free from the inspectors who had formerly taken money from each one. If a man sheared a white sheep, he didn't have to give a share of the wool to a tax collector. When a man divorced his wife, he no longer had to pay a special fee for the privilege. In the days of the corrupt rulers even a dead man wasn't free from the greedy tax collector, who was there with his hand out, expecting a large share of the man's goods. All this was changed by Urukagina: the widow could keep property that had been her husband's.

The temple, too, was restored to its former power and glory. As the ancient document states, "There was no tax collector" in all of Lagash, for Urukagina had "established the freedom" of the people. But his reforms were not set down as a formal code of laws; historians wrote accounts of what had happened during Urukagina's brief ten years on the throne. The number of times these were copied shows that amargi was as exciting an idea to the Sumerians as it is to us today.

The first formal code of laws was established when Ur-Nammu was king of Ur, about 2050 B.C. The story of how he came to the throne and set up what is now the oldest formal law code in the world is told on a small sunbaked clay tablet about eight by four inches in size. Much of the text is worn away, but enough remains to tell us that the scribe divided the tablet into eight columns with each column containing some forty-five ruled lines.   In this cramped space the scribe began his account with a prologue which told how Ur-Nammu was chosen to reign in Ur.

Once the world was created the two high gods of Sumer, An and Enlil, decided to appoint the moon god, Nanna, as king of Ur. Naturally Nanna couldn't be expected to do the heavy work of actual ruling, so he in turn chose Ur-Nammu to act as his representative on earth.   Evidently Ur and all of Sumer were in a state of political upheaval at the time and one of Ur-Nammu's first acts was to settle matters with the neighboring city of Lagash.   He defeated Lagash in battle, killed its kings and, armed "with the power of Nanna, the king of the city," tightened the boundary lines of Ur.

Once he had put Lagash in her place and restored peace, Ur-Nammu turned his attention to the chaotic state of affairs within Ur itself.   Both social and moral reforms were badly needed and the good king, as the documents relate, removed the "grabbers" of the citizens' sheep, oxen, and goats.   Chiselers and grafters were rampant in those early days and Ur-Nammu was one of the first to try to exercise some control over them by instituting a system of honest weights and measures. Nor did he forget the people themselves, for "the widow did not fall prey to the powerful, the orphan did not fall prey to the wealthy" and "the man with one shekel did not fall prey to the man with sixty shekels."

The actual laws were written on the other side of the tablet, but the cuneiform script is so badly worn away, only a few of them can be translated with any degree of clarity.   These, however, indicate that Ur-Nammu had a humane approach to letting "the punishment fit the crime."   One law, literally translated from the old text, apparently deals with a man who had "the foot cut off . . . with an . . . instrument." The perpetrator of this violence did not have his own foot cut off as punishment, but "ten silver shekels he shall pay" to his victim.

Should the amount of the fine be any indication, another law

Ur-Ningirsu was the son and heir of Gudea, governor of Lagash. The head and the body were not part of the same statue. Louvre.

shows that the criminal must have severed several bones at the very least. "If a man to a man with a weapon his bones . . . severed, one silver mina [60 shekels] he shall pay." The phrase "a man to a man" occurs in each of the laws which have been translated and obviously refers to the criminal as the first man and the victim as the second. Another law is equally explicit and indicates that a man's nose was thought to be more valuable than his foot. "If a man to a man with a *geshpu*-instrument that nose has cut off, two thirds of a silver mina [40 shekels] he shall pay." Exactly what a geshpu-instrument was, it is difficult to say, but it must have been well-honed.

Ur-Nammu set a precedent in having his reforms written down. Two hundred years later another king, Lipit-Ishtar, who ruled in Isin, established a more formal code. Several fragments of a large tablet on which his laws were inscribed were found at Nippur. Lipit-Ishtar's code was set up just as Ur-Nammu's was, with a prologue stating his objectives, the laws themselves, then an epilogue announcing that the king has set up his stele for the "well-being" of the people, and that he blesses those who preserve it and curses those who harm it.

Just as they had for Ur-Nammu, the two high gods of Sumer, An and Enlil, "called Lipit-Ishtar . . . the wise shepherd . . . to the princeship of the land in order to establish justice, to turn back complaints [and] . . . to bring well-being to the Sumerians. . . ." The new king then goes on to claim that "I, Lipit-Ishtar . . . procured the freedom of the sons and daughters of Sumer . . . made the father support his children . . . made the children stand by their father. . . ."

As for the laws themselves, only about half of those inscribed on the old tablets are legible, but they are very clear in describing a crime and the fine or punishment that accompanies it. Lipit-Ishtar tried to cover every possible situation in his laws, for they treat matters as diverse as trespass in another man's orchards, real estate sales, death taxes, and runaway slaves. He even paid attention to such details as the man who "rented an ox [and] damaged its eye . . . he shall pay one half of [its] price." But the man who "rented an ox and damaged its tail, he shall pay one fourth of its price," proof once again that everything had its price in ancient Sumer.

The epilogue is even specific about the blessing or curse it pronounces. "May he who will not write his own name upon it [the stele] be presented with life and breath of long days . . . may Enlil's bright forehead look down upon him." Evidently those "fools who write their names in public places" were as common in the early days as they are now and Enlil's bright forehead must have darkened considerably over the centuries.

Lipit-Ishtar had to be explicit in naming each misdemeanor or crime and dictating its punishment, for the law of Sumer was not built on legal precedent as our present law is. Even the judge's decision in the "Case of the Silent Wife" was not recorded as a guideline for any later trial involving a similar situation, as would be done today. Fortunately the Sumerians were dedicated record-keepers and thousands of tablets inscribed with contracts, wills, real estate deals, and legal receipts have been uncovered, particularly in Lagash.

Record-keeping was considered so important that advanced students in the schools spent much of their time copying legal documents in order to become familiar with the terminology of the courts. This must be the reason so many copies of certain codes and court records have been found. These records were called *ditillas,* which means finished lawsuits. Once inscribed, they were wrapped in a clay envelope, marked and carefully filed in the archives. Some of the records found at Lagash involve matters as important as marriage and divorce contracts, inheritances and the sale of property. Others concern legalities such as the appointment of court officials, notarizing the sale of a small amount of barley or hiring a boat. Once an agreement or contract was inscribed on clay there was no room for argument. The methodical Sumerians kept their records in chronological order and filed them away so they were available in case of later dispute.

Apparently, kings who ruled over a wide domain, such as Ur-Nammu and Lipit-Ishtar, were responsible for the laws they made. But in actual practice the local ruler, the ensi, of each city-state saw that they were carried out. The old records were signed by the ensi, along with the judges who decided the case. Each court had three or four such judges. These were not men trained in the law as they are today, however. Being a judge was evidently a part-time job. Merchants, temple administrators, scribes, and inspectors, the important men of the day, served as judges. They probably took turns at such duty very much as jurors do now. But they were powerful and their decisions were final.

The courts followed a set procedure; oaths were taken from witnesses, written documents were produced as evidence and statements were taken from both parties. All this procedure was managed by a man called a *mashkim,* who was evidently a kind of court clerk or bailiff. It was the mashkim who prepared the case for the court and saw to it that the witnesses on both sides were sworn in and all the evidence duly given. Even the mashkims were not men trained to the job as a pro-

A treaty of brotherhood between Lagash and Erech is inscribed on this vessel. British Museum.

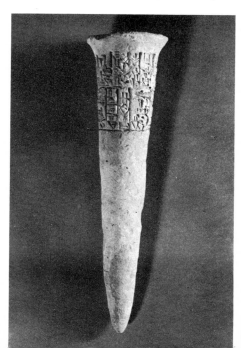

fession. The old records show, however, that they were men of standing in the community, probably appointed by the ensi to serve a term for the courts. They were sometimes paid for such service; one document states "One shekel of silver and one lamb were payment for what the mashkim did."

A typical ditilla, found in the archives at Lagash, is interesting as proof that the women of Sumer had property rights and power over their own money. A partial translation of the old tablet reads:

> Innashagga, wife of Dudu . . . bought a . . . house . . . with her own money. As long as Dudu lived, Ur-Eninnu, the son of Dudu, had possession of his house. Since Innashagga had bought the house, he [Ur-Eninnu] had the tablet recording the purchase of the house, made over to him by Innashagga. Innashagga took the oath that she had bought the house with her own money and not with [that] of Dudu . . . Therefore . . . the house [was] confirmed as belonging to Innashagga, the wife of Dudu . . . The heirs swore by the name of their king that they would not change their mother's word.

The document was signed by the mashkim and three of "their judges."

Today women in certain countries of the world, having no such rights over their own money and property, might well envy the Sumerian women who lived under the enlightened laws of Lipit-Ishtar. For Lipit-Ishtar was seriously concerned with the freedom of his people and had a right to claim, as he did in the prologue to his code, that he had "established justice in Sumer . . . in accordance with the word of Enlil." Over the long pull of the following centuries it is freedom, the amargi of the ancient Sumerians, that has been man's highest dream and his best hope that Enlil's "bright forehead" may continue to shine upon mankind.

Stele of Naram-sin shows his troops winning a great victory. Louvre.

chapter 9

ARTS IN SUMER

NEARLY 5,000 years ago the lady Shubad lay down to die in a stone chamber with a crown of golden leaves upon her head. Affixed to this headdress was a beaded wreath with a high silver comb decorated with flowers of gold and lapis lazuli. Heavy hoops of gold hung from her ears, and around her throat was a necklace of gold and lapis lazuli. She wore a garment intricately designed with beads, gold, silver, carnelian, and chalcedony. Near her hand was a golden cup which archaeologists suspect contained the poison that sent her to her death.

Shubad's grave was discovered by Sir Leonard Woolley in the late 1920s. Nothing like these products of the goldsmith's art had been found in other digs in Sumer and nothing like them has been found since. Graverobbers throughout the centuries took care of that. But the Royal Cemeteries at Ur were deep underground. The thieves never found the jewelry and golden ornaments which testify so strikingly to the craftsmanship of the Sumerian goldsmith.

Since so much that is representative of the jeweler's and sculptor's work was found when Sir Leonard Woolley uncovered the Royal Cemeteries at Ur and the nearby mound at

128

Golden helmet is from Ur. Museum of Baghdad.

al-Ubaid, a brief account of his work gives the clearest idea of this flowering of Sumerian art. In 1922 Sir Leonard led a joint British and American expedition to the southern plains of Sumer, hoping to "recover monuments taking us back so far in time as the reign of Ur-Nammu, founder of the Third Dynasty of Ur," and the man who established the first formal law code in Sumer. "King Ur-Nammu," as Sir Leonard wrote, "was indeed almost the first character in the history of Mesopotamia to be acknowledged by scholars to be historically authentic." * These scholars and Sir Leonard himself had little hope of finding anything that would establish a king or dynasty any earlier than that of Ur-Nammu.

But almost at once, in digging near the mound at al-Ubaid, a settlement far older than the nearby city of Ur, Sir Leonard came upon the ruins of a temple dating from the First Dynasty

*Sir Leonard Woolley, *Excavations at Ur.*

Golden cup of Lady Shubad which may once have contained poison, was found in the Royal Cemetery of Ur. British Museum.

of Ur. ". . . a workman unearthed before my eyes a small oblong tablet of white limestone bearing an inscription. . . ." Translated, it read: "A-anni-pad-da King of Ur, son of Mes-anni-pad-da King of Ur, has built this for his lady, Ninhursag," the mother goddess of the Sumerians. The tablet itself "was the foundation stone of the building and most important of all our discoveries."

The tablet was important because Mes-anni-pad-da appears on the King Lists as the first king of the First Dynasty of Ur. This pushed history back to about 2700 B.C. and gave the archaeologists a specific date for the temple and the objects found within it. A huge copper relief of eagles and lions had once risen high above the gateway to the temple. Reliefs of the same metal adorned the walls and four enormous copper bulls stood somewhere within the enclosure. Great columns, decorated with mosaics of colored stone or sheathed in beaten copper, once held high its walls.

The most interesting frieze, with figures carved from shell and white limestone and inlaid on shale between bands of copper, shows the priests of the temple milking the sacred cows, which represented the mother goddess Ninhursag, for this milk was "the nourishment of kings." The frieze shows the cows being milked from behind while the calves stand by, wearing muzzles.   A reed barn stands in the center of the scene, while to the left a priest pours milk through a funnel as others make butter in huge jars.   All in all, it gives a graphic picture of a Sumerian dairy farm.

This ancient temple, the oldest in the world at the time of its discovery, evidently was sacked during one of the violent wars that racked Sumer throughout its history.   Its columns were flung down.   The vandals "collected the bull statues in a heap and had undercut the walls and toppled them over."   But Ninhursag's temple rose once again from the dust.   Its remains now stand as the finest example of the very early art and architecture of Sumer.

A few miles to the south of al-Ubaid was the huge mound where the great city of Ur had once stood.   During the first years of digging, Sir Leonard had discovered graves there containing a scattering of gold beads.   He suspected that greater treasures lay buried beneath the packed sand, treasures that might predate those of al-Ubaid. But Sir Leonard was a scientist and, as he said, "Our object was to get history, not fill museums with miscellaneous curios."   In these early days of the expedition he "had a force of very wild Arab tribesmen, few of whom had ever handled tools before."

He decided to wait to begin serious excavating at the mound of Ur until he could train these workmen.   By 1927 he had brought them to such a pitch of perfection that he could write:

> Of course their main incentive is money, [but] they know that our object is . . . a search for some mysterious knowledge and a workman digging at a barren spot . . . may be heard to comfort himself with the muttered phrase "this is in the interest of science." . . .   The best of them acquire a very great manual dexterity in the use of the entrenching tool and the knife and will seldom do damage to the most delicate object.

The first site chosen as a dig was a cemetery which lay inside the wall of a temple built at a much later period. In the upper layer of this vast graveyard were more than eighteen hundred graves, none of which contained anything of real value, only the bones of the forgotten dead. But among these graves were deep tunnels, evidently dug by robbers centuries earlier. They seemed an indication that greater treasures might lie below.

The first real find was the tomb of a man, identified by a seal as Mes-kalam-dug, who had lived about 2500 B.C. His skull still wore a helmet, hammered from one sheet of gold alloy and shaped like a wig with the hair tied in a knot at the back. The gold headpiece was beautifully chased to show wavy hair; a circlet held it in place and gold loops went over the ears. Holes around the edges once held laces tied to a padded lining. The workmanship and simple detail make this the finest example of Sumerian goldwork yet found beneath the sand. Gold-mounted daggers, an embossed shield, and copper, silver, and stone bowls lay beside him. At his side was a golden dagger and the bones of his hands still held a bowl of heavy gold over what must once have been a shield made of hundreds of beads of gold and lapis lazuli. Sir Leonard did not exaggerate when he said that "nothing like these things had ever before come from the soil of Mesopotamia."

But even more exciting discoveries lay ahead. In excavating another shaft nearby, the workmen came upon blocks of limestone forming a pavement. Since there was no natural stone in the area, the limestone must have been imported to line the entrance to a royal tomb.

Although a tunnel dug into the area proved that graverobbers had been here before, the workmen kept at their digging, hoping for a find the marauders might have overlooked. Their industry was rewarded with the discovery of five skeletons carefully arranged in a sloping trench. "They wore headdresses of gold, lapis lazuli and elaborate bead necklaces. . . . At the end of the row lay the remains of a wonderful harp [and] across the

ruins of the harp lay the bones of the gold-crowned harpist."
Scattered in the dust were animal bones, the remains of a
chariot emblazoned with gold lions and colored stones, a gam-
ing board, copper vessels, a golden saw, and chests whose wood
had decayed but whose mosaic decorations still remained.   A
multitude of "tall, slender silver tumblers nested one inside the
other; a similar tumbler of gold, fluted and chased . . . a chalice
. . . lay piled together [with] two magnificent lions' heads of
silver. . . ."

But "all this wealth of objects" could not be identified as

A bull, cast in copper.   British
Museum.

belonging to any one of the skeletons found within the pit, except for a man named A-bar-gi, whose tomb contained a seal bearing his name. His identity was never recorded in Sumerian history, but he must have been a man of importance. Those who robbed his tomb left behind two small boats, one of copper and the other of silver. The ramp leading up to A-bar-gi's tomb contained a treasure house of objects and a small army of skeletons. Six soldiers, their spears beside them and copper helmets on their heads, lay in two rows at the top of the ramp. Wagons, crumbled into dust, but with the skeletons of the oxen and their drivers still intact, lay at the bottom of the slope near the stone chamber. Beside the wall of this tomb were the skeletal remains of nine women with the shreds of brightly colored robes clinging to their bones. Headdresses of lapis lazuli and carnelian had once adorned their heads; golden earrings and necklaces of bright stones lay among the dust and bones. Sir Leonard wrote:

> The whole space between them and the wagons was crowded with other dead, women and men, while the passage which led along the side of the stone chamber was lined with soldiers carrying daggers, and with women . . . On top of the bodies of the "court ladies" against the chamber wall had been placed a wooden harp . . . by the side of the wall of the pit was a second harp with a wonderful bull's head in gold, its eyes, beard and horn tips of lapis-lazuli, and a set of engraved shell plaques no less wonderful; there are four of them, with grotesque scenes of animals playing the parts of men.*

Above A-bar-gi's tomb the excavators came upon one that the robbers had somehow overlooked. This was where Shubad, either queen or high priestess, had lain down to die with an exquisite crown of golden leaves upon her head. Sir Leonard

*Sir Leonard Woolley, *Ur of the Chaldees*.

describes her as he first found her: ". . . inside the chamber
. . . lay the body of Queen Shubad [an inscribed cylinder found
nearby gave her name].   She lay quite straight on her back . . .
her hands crossed over her stomach; a woman attendant was
crouched by the side of the bier, near the head, and a second
at the foot."*

Lady Woolley, a skillful artist, modeled a head in wax on
the skull of another skeleton found nearby, for Shubad's bones
had crumbled to dust.   On it she mounted a dark wig which
she crowned with the glorious wreath of leaves and jeweled
sprays which had been picked from the rubble and carefully
fitted together.   Later students felt that Lady Woolley made
a mistake in placing the crown so low on Shubad's forehead.
Sumerian women of rank wore their hair coiled high.   Perhaps
Shubad's headdress was meant to fit this crown of hair and to
allow the delicate leaves and golden circles to dangle gracefully
above her forehead.

But such speculation seems trivial in the face of the contro-
versy among scholars over who Shubad really was and how and
why she died.   Sir Leonard referred to her as a queen.   But
she died about 3000 B.C., before the King Lists record the local
rulers of Ur, so there is no real evidence of her regal status.
Others feel she must have been a high priestess who died during
a religious ceremony that required a sacrifice to the gods.   The
metal cups found near each skeleton, those of Shubad and of
all the attendants along the ramp leading to her tomb, suggest
the latter theory.

There was no evidence of violent struggle in any of the Death
Pits Sir Leonard found at Ur.

The rich garments and elaborate jewelry of the women,
the military accoutrements of the men, the splendidly
mounted chariots and wagons—all suggest that these were

---

*Sir Leonard Woolley, *Ur Excavations; the Royal Cemetery.*

people of rank, and that they had gone to their deaths voluntarily. An elaborate religious ceremony must have taken place before the interment, with much music and chanting. "In one case," recorded Woolley, "the harpist had continued playing to the last, her fingers still outstretched across the strings of her instrument. In another grave it was clear that, after the attendants had become unconscious, people had entered the death pit, killed the animals and placed the harp *above* the inert body of its player."*

In another Death Pit Woolley uncovered pathetic evidence that one of the victims was not ready to die. In this mass grave were the bodies of sixty-four women and six men, lying in rows along the ramp. All the women but one had worn gold or silver headbands. Beside the skeleton of this one attendant was a tightly rolled bit of metal. Apparently she had kept the silver circlet clutched in her hand or in a pocket of her robe and hadn't had time to put it on. Perhaps she had just forgotten this last ceremonial act.

The discoveries at Ur are by far the most dramatic and artistically notable of all the treasure dug from the sands of Sumer. But an enormous variety of art and artifacts has come from the Land between the Rivers. Most closely associated with the Sumerians are the cylinder seals. In the very earliest times, when the art of writing was just developing, these seals were stone beads, cut with a simple pictorial sign and used by a special person as an identifying mark. Later, they were made from precious and durable stones which were far more elaborately and expertly carved. Rolled over a piece of soft clay, they left an impression which not only identified the owner of the seal, but provided vivid pictures of many phases of social, economic, and religious life. The early seals were far more original and creative than those of later periods, for the crafts-

*Leonard Cottrell, *The Quest for Sumer.*

men used a high degree of imagination in inventing designs that suited the man for whom the seal was being made. Into the tiny stone cylinders they cut a delightful variety of fairy-tale animals, monsters and mythical creatures, each one related in some way to the personality of the owner. They carved, for example, a shepherd defending his fold against wild beasts, a king receiving homage from his subjects, or a scribe with his tablet.

The gods never could be neglected. An enormous array of seals have been found, showing these lofty ones performing virtuous acts or seated in splendor before their attendants and worshippers. Such seals were dedicated by their owners to the god pictured thereon; a small space was left free for that owner's

This statue, found in the temple dedicated to Ishtar at Mari, has an unusually appealing face. Museum of Damascus.

identifying mark.   Later the seals became more formalized and showed a simple, quite modern design of leaves, scrolls and whirls, again with a space left for the owner's name.   In the later period of the Sumerian seal the process of standardization made it a uniform design, one showing a worshipper (the owner) being presented to a god such as Enlil by his personal god or "good angel."

Most of the statuary in the round (as opposed to the bas-reliefs) found in the sand heaps of the old cities was also of a religious nature.   When a king or more humble mortal had his image reproduced in stone, he was almost always portrayed in an attitude of worship to show the subject's adoration of the gods.   A woman's figure, simply cut in gypsum, was found at Nippur, where it had evidently stood before a temple altar. The wooden head with its staring eyes had once been covered with a gold mask.   The statue's hands are folded in prayer.

Several figurines discovered near the altar of the temple at Tell Asmar, one of the northern cities of Sumer, depict an entire group of worshippers.   The rudely modeled, blocky stone stat- uettes with their huge round eyes, curled beards, and folded hands represent ordinary devotees.   The two taller figures are certainly gods; the clean-shaven man is a priest.   They give some idea of what the Sumerians looked like: rather chunky and solid, the practical men of the ancient world.

The thirty-odd statues of Gudea, governor of Lagash, show him as a stolid, square character.   Gudea's statues, some only a head, others a full seated figure, were carved from diorite, a very hard stone, then polished to a high degree of brilliance. Formalized as they are, they are skillfully executed, a consid- erable feat in view of the hardness of the stone.

Gudea, who ruled in the days when Lagash was the most powerful city-state in Sumer, was a calculating builder.   He knew well that his power and also his hope of survival depended on Ningirsu, the chief deity of Lagash and a god high in the sacred register.   A detailed account, written in the twenty-second century B.C., tells how Gudea had a dream in which he was instructed to build a magnificent temple for Ningirsu out of ebony and logs of cedar from distant lands. Gudea himself made the first brick with formal ceremonies, displaying it to his subjects "like a pure crown lifted to the sky." One seated statue shows Gudea with the plan of the temple resting on his lap. All these statues were meant to act as mediators between Gudea and Ningirsu. "Statue, say to my king [god] . . ." Gudea admonishes one of these stone figures.

Among the relatively few statues of known historical characters is a dramatically arrogant bronze head which many experts feel is that of Sargon I in the days of his glory. Even though the eyes, once made of valuable stone, were long ago gouged out by robbers, the head, larger than life size, with its curled beard and sneering lips, gives a powerful impression of the great king. Dudu, a scribe, had himself portrayed seated in prayerful attitude, making an offering to his god. This is one of the few statues that shows a figure seated; the bunchy skirts the Sumerians wore didn't lend themselves to a graceful pose in this position. Even the seated Gudea's robes seem awkward, although arranged in a simpler way.

When the Inanna Temple was excavated at Nippur the foundation box, containing objects relating to the time it was built, just as a modern cornerstone does, held a variety of small copper and stone statues. A roughly modeled head of an unknown woman, perhaps a priestess, was one of the finds. A smaller copper statue, however, was even more interesting. It represents Ur-Nammu, the builder of the temple, for at that time, around 2050 B.C., Ur-Nammu was ruler of all Sumer. Naturally, he busied himself in building temples to convince the ruling deity of each city-state that he was deeply conscious of the god's importance. Ur-Nammu's face is more finely formed than that of the unknown woman. It shows a thoughtful man, quite in keeping with his reputation as a law-giver and dispenser of justice.

The most domestic of all the statues is one found at Nippur which shows a seated couple, in a beguiling portrait of marital happiness. Although the figures are crudely formed, with little attempt to delineate the folds of their garments or the shape of their bodies, they are touchingly human and real.

By far the loveliest of the Sumerian portraits in stone is one of an unnamed lady found at Uruk, a city-state that flourished in the earliest days of Sumer's history. The head is of marble and beautifully modeled with a fine sense of line and form. Once her sightless eyes and straight eyebrows were inlaid with colored stones, but they were long ago stolen from the marble. On her head was an engraved copper or gold headdress, also ripped away by thieves. But even without these adornments, the serene marble face has a beauty far superior to most Sumerian sculpture.

Animals were a favorite subject of Sumerian art. Many plaques, reliefs, seals, and carved vases depict domestic animals—placid cows, sheep, or donkeys. Others portray lions or other wild beasts, often shown taking a bite out of an unfortunate victim. It was natural that domestic animals, so important to Sumerian economy, should be depicted with such great frequency. The wild beasts, however, had a special significance as a reminder of man's need for the protection of the gods. A carved shell, for instance, shows a lion attacking a bull, the eyes of both animals wide open in the same state of mild surprise. Such figures were done simply but they have a vigor that suits the subject.

A miniature copper chariot, dating from about 2700 B.C., pictures a driver guiding four donkeys and gives an idea of the war vehicles of that era. The artist, even in these rough-hewn figures, was able to infuse the small animals with spirit and vitality. Donkeys were apparently a favorite subject for sculptors, perhaps as an expression of gratitude for their patient service to the Sumerians.

One of the finest treasures dug from the Royal Cemeteries

is the gold and lapis-lazuli goat standing erect among the branches of a golden tree. Twenty inches high, the face, legs, and central core were made of wood. But after 5,000 years beneath some thirty feet of earth, the wood had completely disintegrated; only the broken gold leaf, the bits of lapis and shell were left. The impressions left in the packed earth were clear enough to show the restorers how this extraordinary goat once looked. He was brought to life again, a powerful image that reflects, together with the bearded bull, the highest form of the Sumerian goldsmith's art.

Often animals were shown as creatures of fantasy: beasts were described in Sumerian literature as "the great lion demon" or

Gold and lapis-lazuli statue of a goat from the Royal Cemetery at Ur. University Museum of Philadelphia.

Bronze lion was the custodian of a Babylonian temple. Museum of Aleppo.

"the monstrous pig." Bulls were given human faces and eagles, a lion's head. Wild beasts also performed human activities in Sumerian art; they played harps or served guests at a banquet. Naturally, animals played a part in religion, aside from their very fundamental role as sacrificial offerings. Images of bulls and goats were thought to insure fertility and were used to guard a man's house. Small clay statues of dogs were buried under the doorstep of a house to protect its owner. The Sumerians had a strong sense of an animal's relationship to mankind and their pictured and sculptured forms are often done with more feeling than are human figures.

The stele, a huge slab of stone, was a favorite device whereby a ruler commemorated his deeds and accomplishments. It also afforded an artist a chance to portray figures in action. Ur-Nammu had a stele cut in limestone to glorify his part in building the Temple of the Moon God at Ur. The god Nanna appears at the top of the stele with the moon curved over his head. Just below, Ur-Nammu is receiving a parade of priests

142

who are performing ritual acts of worship. The bottom of the stele shows the actual building of the temple. A great many plaques and foundation stones have been found near the old temples, all of them praising a ruler's piety for having built ziggurats.

Other steles were erected for more ordinary reasons: to show a king's temporal power or to glorify his warlike deeds. The Stele of the Vultures is an outstanding example of this form of self-aggrandizement. The limestone monument, over six feet in height, was erected about 2400 B.C. by Eannatum, ruler of Lagash, to commemorate his victory over the neighboring city of Umma.

The scene is set forth in elaborate detail. In the upper left of the stele, Eannatum is leading into battle a group of spearmen, protected by shields, and trampling an enemy horde beneath their feet. The place of honor is reserved for Ningirsu, who, as chief god of Lagash, was naturally responsible for the victory. He is holding a net filled with unhappy Ummaites, one of whom he is in the act of subduing with a heavy club. At the bottom of the stele is another company of spearmen, following a charioteer into the fray.

Naram-Sin, Sargon's grandson, who made the fatal mistake of sacking Nippur, claimed the title King of the Four Quarters of the World and allowed himself to be worshipped as a god. On a stele of pink limestone he is wearing a god's horned helmet as he stands at the base of a cone-shaped mountain with two of his enemies on their knees in front of him, begging for mercy. Other victims, praying, falling to their death, or already crushed by the might of Naram-Sin, are scattered along the base. Of course, Naram-Sin is shown as twice the size of his foes, but even he must pay due respect to the gods who made his victory possible. Their stars shine above the mountain peak. These active and dramatic figures, carved about 2300 B.C., during the reign of Naram-Sin, are effectively designed to fill the shape of the stele. Yet each line, the direction of each

This is part of the battle scene appearing in the Royal Standard of Ur. British Museum.

man's eyes, is upward toward Naram-Sin and the stars of the gods above him.

Life in Sumer, however, was not all battles and violence as the Royal Standard found at Ur shows. War and peace seemed to go hand in hand in these early days. This intricate mosaic adorned a box twenty-two inches long. One side of the box gives a vivid picture of a conquering army as the king leads it into battle in his chariot, crunching the fallen enemy under its wheels. As a detailed picture of a Sumerian army on the march, this panel of the Royal Standard cannot be matched in any other contemporary battle scene.

The other side of the box, however, shows the victory banquet, a scene of comparative tranquillity that tells a good deal

144

about life in the higher social circles of Sumer. At the upper
left of the top row of pictures the king is enthroned, larger than
the officers who face him. The latter are apparently toasting
the king, for each one holds high a goblet. Off to the right
is a female singer, accompanied by a harpist whose instrument
is decorated with a bull's head. In other scenes on the victory
panel animals and fish are being carried to the feast, and teams
of donkeys and bearers transport the booty won from the enemy.

A bull's head, such as the one shown in the scene on the

A bull's head decorates a harp from the Royal Cemetery at Ur.
University Museum of Philadelphia.

mosaic box, was often depicted in Sumerian art, for the bull was a symbol of strength and power. A truly incredible harp with a bearded bull's head of lapis lazuli and gold was found in the Royal Cemetery at Ur. Although it had been smashed to bits, the gold and lapis, the inlaid plaques of animals and mythological figures were carefully reassembled and the extraordinary creation was affixed once more to the sound-box of a wooden harp. The bull's head is so arrogant the fact that it has a beard does not seem at all extraordinary.

Victory feasts such as the one shown on the Royal Standard would naturally be celebrated with song and harp, but music played an important role in many phases of ordinary life. A "dispute," translated from an old tablet, shows what one Sumerian thought of another's musical talents.

You have a harp, but know no music . . .
Your throat can't sound a note . . .
[You] can't sing a hymn, can't open your mouth
And you are an accomplished fellow!

Harps, lyres, pipes, and drums have been found in many of the old tombs. All these instruments must have been used to accompany singers. The innumerable hymns and songs, translated from cuneiform documents, are further proof that music, both vocal and instrumental, was a lively art form in Sumer. Dancing must often have accompanied the music and singing, certainly as a form of worship in the temples. For music, then as now, was an integral part of religious celebration.

It is difficult and probably unfair to judge the Sumerians' artistic achievement. The thieves who broke into the ancient palaces and despoiled the tombs left only those objects which had no ready sales value. The stiff little stone and clay figures of priests, gods, and laymen, all so much alike, have been found in all the digs. They were probably turned out by the thousands in the shops of the image makers, very much as the plaster models of saints are made in today's art factories.

If the figures had eyes or decorations of precious or semi-precious stones, they were ripped out and sold. Few examples of statuary of real merit escaped the graverobbers. The exquisite marble head of a woman found at Erech, the carefully executed statues of Gudea, and the fierce power of Sargon's head give a tantalizing suggestion of what the Sumerians must have accomplished as sculptors.

The metalworkers' skill is more easily appraised. The lucky chance that saved the Royal Cemeteries at Ur from the graverobbers has preserved some marvelous examples of their work. Shubad's jewelry, the imaginative artistry of the goat in the thicket, and the bull's head harp are evidence enough of the high art attained by these ancient goldsmiths.

It was as architects, however, that the Sumerians reached their peak of artistic achievement. Considering the material with which they had to work (mud baked into bricks), they showed extraordinary creativity and imagination in building domes, arches, and vaults. Most private houses, palaces, and public buildings have long since crumbled into the dust of centuries. But the remains of many magnificent temples have been uncovered, so it is now possible for these edifices to be reconstructed.

Since the worship of the gods was a Sumerian's first duty, the temple, which housed a city's special god, was the very soul and center of his life. These temples followed the same general plan, although the earliest ones were smaller and simpler in design than later ones. The Sumerians erected their houses of worship on a mound to bring them nearer to heaven, for these temples were to act as the "bond between heaven and earth."

Sumer was a flat land, so the temple builders first constructed a vast foundation of mud brick or stone on which they built a massive staged tower, the *ziggurat,* to serve as the connecting link between earth and heaven. A stairway led up the outside of the ziggurat to the shrine where the god dwelt. An early shrine excavated at Eridu was very simply designed in a small rectangle, but even this one contained a niche for the god's image and an offering table of mud brick before it. Later the temple was enlarged to make room for several antechambers surrounding the shrine and buttresses were added to support the larger walls.

Archaeologists believe that the temple at Erech was built about 3000 B.C. on a mound some forty feet high. The mud-brick walls were decorated with clay cones, dipped in black, red, and buff colors and arranged in geometric patterns. Columns were added and these, too, were covered with the same cone decorations.

The best preserved of all the ruined temples in Sumer is the Temple for the Moon God, Nanna, built by Ur-Nammu at Ur. It "contained the ziggurat as well as a large number of shrines, storehouses, magazines, courtyards, and dwelling places for the temple personnel. The ziggurat, the outstanding feature, was a rectangular tower whose . . . original height was about seventy feet. The whole was a solid mass of brick work with a cover of crude mud bricks and an outer layer of burnt bricks set in bitumen [natural asphalt]."*

Architecture throughout the ages owes its infinite variety to these early Sumerian designers. The ziggurat itself was copied and recopied throughout the following centuries. It reached its highest form in the Hanging Gardens of Babylon, built in the sixth century B.C. by Nebuchadnezzar. Rising seventy-five feet above the plain, the gardens were planted with trees and shrubs and watered by an intricate hydraulic system.

But the temple at Ur must have been the wonder of the Sumerian world, for the great god of the air, Enlil, gave his blessing to it:

City whose fate has been decreed by Enlil,
Shrine Ur, may you rise heaven high.

*Samuel Noah Kramer, *The Sumerians.*

chapter 10

THE SUMERIAN SCIENTIST

Sift and knead together—all in one—turtle shell, the sprouting naga-plant, salt [and] mustard; wash [the sick part] with quality beer [and] hot water; scrub [the sick spot] with all of it [the kneaded mixture]: after scrubbing, rub with vegetable oil [and] cover with pulverized fir.

T HE physician who wrote this prescription for an unknown disease lived 4000 years ago. Since he compiled fifteen such prescriptions on a small tablet, roughly 4 by 6 inches in size, he must have had some assurance that his nostrum, even the pulverized fir, was an effective remedy for whatever ailed his patient.

In any case, this remarkable medical handbook, excavated from the ruins of Nippur nearly seventy years ago, is, so far as we know, the oldest in the world. Its translation was especially difficult, for it contained technical phrases with which cuneiform scholars were unfamiliar. But Professor Kramer, with the aid of a chemistry student, was able in 1953 to translate the old document. From it he could deduce that the Sumerians had a practical approach to the study and theory of medicine.

This tablet contained no magic incantations to drive out the demons that most ancient peoples were convinced caused diseases. Instead, its prescriptions were carefully compounded. The Sumerian doctor who wrote this handbook used materials from nature for his salves and medicines. The minerals were mostly salt or saltpeter; for some of his prescriptions he boiled, filtered, and pulverized snakeskin or turtle shell and milk. But by far the larger part of his ingredients came from plants: cassia, myrtle, and thyme.   The seeds, roots, and bark of trees such as the willow, pear, fig, and date palm were made into powder, then mixed with wine, beer, or plant oils.   Even river clay was dried and kneaded with honey to form a salve.

With each of his remedies the physician gave careful instructions for use.   In the case of a salve, the afflicted person must first rub the ailing part with oil, then "fasten as a poultice" the prescribed mixture.   Evidently beer was used as a means of making the medicines more palatable, for several remedies direct the patient to "put the [pulverized simple] in beer and let the sick man drink."

The physician who composed this document made a special effort to have his patients understand his directions.   He wrote in a large and rather elegant hand, creating a cuneiform tablet that is unusually clear.   He also had some idea of the need for cleanliness in caring for his patients.   Almost every prescription directs that the "sick spot" be "washed" or "scrubbed."   In spite of all his care, however, he neglected to state what each remedy was meant to cure or how much of it was to be used. The first twenty-one lines of the old script are too badly damaged to be translated and perhaps he wrote a list of ailments as a preface to his handbook.

A more likely reason for not mentioning specific diseases may be that this learned doctor was a teacher in a Sumerian medical school.   If this were the case, he might well describe the ailments and the dosage for each in talking to his students. Certainly he was well educated, as shown by his knowledge of technical terms and his skill with the reed stylus.

In Sumer a doctor was known as the *a-zu*, which means water-knower, and he enjoyed a position of respect in the community.   A man named Lulu is the first physician mentioned by name in recorded history.   He is listed on a tablet found at Ur and written about 2700 B.C.   Other old texts refer to a "doctor of donkeys" or a "doctor of the oxen," indicating that there were also veterinarians. But, so far, no further reference to them has been found.

The Sumerians must have had considerable skill as surgeons. Several skulls found in the old graves show evidence of having been trepanned (cut through the bone), perhaps to relieve pressure on the brain. Knives, lancets, and forceps have been discovered. There is, however, no reference in any of the old tablets to the work of a surgeon. Certainly the Sumerians must have had a considerable knowledge of anatomy, for

(Left.) The vine carried by this man symbolizes good wishes. British Museum. (Right.) An astrological tablet of the Babylonian period from Erech. State Museum of Berlin.

they performed elaborate dissections in the ritual sacrifice of animals for religious ceremonies.

The clearest idea of medical science as practiced by the Sumerians is that Nippur tablet with the doctor's specific directions for preparing salves and medicines to cure the sick spots of his patients.

Unlike the down-to-earth physician, most "scientists" of ancient Sumer were priests who ascribed all their knowledge to the gods and were very careful to keep their knowledge to themselves. Except for the scribes, they were the only educated people in Sumer. In order to maintain their position, the priests made a tremendous mystery of their knowledge and its divine sources. As a result, religion and science were inseparable in the mind of the average Sumerian.

The Sumerians' conviction that true learning was untouchable, because the gods had created all things by divine law, kept them from evolving a truly scientific approach to the world. They made no attempt, for instance, to connect the annual rising of the rivers to the melting of the snows in the mountains to the north. As we have seen, the Sumerians had one answer to all natural phenomena: "Enki did it."

The early scientists were practical men in most things, however. They studied the stars and learned from them when to till the fields, plant the grain, and harvest. In fact, every phase of economic and agricultural activity was directed by these priest-scientists, who firmly believed that their interpretation of the stars was divinely inspired.

Before Gudea built his temple at Lagash, a goddess appeared to him in a dream, carrying a tablet on which the stars in the heavens were shown. This dream persuaded the devout ruler that he was to build a temple under the direction of the "holy stars." The fact that Gudea could dream of stars in a certain fixed position proves that the Sumerians must have studied the heavens and drawn certain conclusions about their changing places.

Only about twenty-five stars are listed and named in the old texts. Nevertheless, the Sumerians did invent a calendar. The year was divided into two seasons: *emesh,* summer, which began in what is now February-March; *enten,* the winter period, which started in September-October. Each month lasted twenty-nine or thirty days and began on the evening of the new moon. To account for the lapsed time each year, an extra month was inserted at regular intervals. It is difficult to fix a Sumerian name to any of these months, for they varied in each city-state. But most of them took their names from agricultural activities or feast days for the gods. The day itself began at sunset. The twelve "double-hours" which made up the time between sunsets were calculated by water clocks, which measured time by allowing a specified amount of water to flow through the small opening of a jar. This rough form of astronomy owed its inspiration to the "honored lord," An, as he "sits on the heavenly dais."

The Sumerians were on firmer ground as engineers and mathematicians. Their dependence on their complicated and ingenious system of canals, dikes, and ditches for agriculture has already been mentioned. The planning of this hydraulic feat led them to develop a method of calculating that became their highest scientific achievement. They also needed to measure land boundaries, to plan their massive building operations and to weigh and measure their goods for trade and commerce. Then there were always the tax gatherers, whose unpopular work demanded an accurate accounting.

The time units used today on clocks and watches were first invented by the Sumerians, whose water clocks divided the minute into sixty seconds and the hour into sixty minutes. These ancient mathematicians used arithmetic and the decimal system, multiplication tables, fractions and division. Many of their mathematical problems were inscribed on clay tablets so they could be used in the schools. The Sumerian schoolboy was given such problems as measuring the length or width of canals, counting bricks, or calculating the length and breadth of a field or building. The tables set forth cube and square roots, as well as the areas of rectangles and squares.

But even their knowledge of the intricate uses of numbers could not be attributed to the ingenuity of mere man. The Sumerians believed everything they accomplished had its beginnings with Enki and, through Enki's amazing ability to "budget the accounts of the universe," they laid the foundations of modern astronomy and mathematics. The Babylonians built on this knowledge and other civilizations throughout the ages have reason to be grateful to Enki, he who claimed to be the "ear and mind of all the lands."

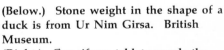

(Below.) Stone weight in the shape of a duck is from Ur Nim Girsa. British Museum.
(Right.) Cuneiform tablet records the flood story in Gilgamesh. British Museum.

(Top.) The hero, Gilgamesh, is shown in a relief from the Palace of Sargon II. Louvre.
(Right.) Gilgamesh, as visualized around 800 BC. Louvre.

156

chapter **11**

EPICS OF GILGAMESH

ARCHITECTS, engineers, artists, and craftsmen—the Sumerians were all of these but it was as writers that they excelled. Not only did they invent a method of writing which, in itself, was an extraordinary achievement, but they also composed poetry, hymns, proverbs, legends, and myths which have a high order of originality and imagination.

Gilgamesh is the supreme Sumerian hero, without fear and above reproach. The tales of his exploits, triumphs, and tragedies have a universal appeal. He is the first of the world's supermen, the model for all those who came after him.

About 2600 B.C., when Gilgamesh became king of Erech, he was already a hero to his people. He was also a man who had no false modesty about himself or his role in life. He described himself as "strong as a savage bull," "most splendid among heroes" and "most glorious among men." Although Gilgamesh was worshipped as a god in his own lifetime, he was thoroughly human. He loved, he hated, he wept, and he rejoiced as all mortal men must.

Gilgamesh had something of a running start for becoming

a hero; his grandfather, Lugalbanda, was himself king of Erech and a legendary hero. His mother was the goddess Ninsun. But Gilgamesh, hereditary king of one of the most powerful city-states of Sumer, was extraordinary in his own right, endowed with unrivaled physical strength, remarkable good looks, and an overpowering desire for fame and adventure.

"Why," asked his mother of the sun god, Utu, "having given me Gilgamesh for a son, with a restless heart didst thou endow him?"

This restless heart also made him a tyrant and bully to his own subjects. The wise mothers of Erech locked up their daughters. No man dared challenge him for fear of incurring his terrible wrath. The people of Erech complained to the gods of Gilgamesh's excesses. Understanding that Gilgamesh behaved as he did because no mortal man could stand against him, the gods in their wisdom decided that what Gilgamesh needed was someone who could be an antagonist, one capable of subduing his arrogant spirit.

Ninhursag, the mother goddess, was directed to fashion such a man from clay and to breathe life into him. The man she created was known as Enkidu, a wild man, a creature of the plains. He had never known human companionship, but had grown up among the beasts, a long-haired and powerful brute. The gods realized that before he could become a worthy adversary for Gilgamesh he must first be civilized.

A woman of Erech was engaged to teach Enkidu the fine arts of eating, drinking, and wearing clothes. She also used her womanly arts to bring his wild spirit under control. What he lost in brute strength, he gained in enhanced spiritual and mental powers. A wise and civilized man at last, as the result of the training, he was ready to come face to face with the mighty Gilgamesh.

Gilgamesh wasn't altogether unprepared for the contest. A dream had warned him of the coming of a rival. He decided that his first duty was to show this upstart that he would brook no other leader in Erech.   Gilgamesh challenged Enkidu to an orgy of eating and drinking.   Whoever remained on his feet after a night of carousing would be proclaimed the winner.

The two men met outside the appointed house.   Enkidu immediately showed the effects of his teaching.   Obviously feeling that such a competition was beneath their dignity as heroes, he objected to entering the place and tried to prevent Gilgamesh from going in as well.   Gilgamesh was filled with wrath at such temerity.   The two great men drew their swords and began to fight.

Unfortunately the tablet from which this battle of titans is translated is worn away at this most interesting moment and doesn't become clear again until the battle was well under way. At this point, Enkidu, the man of the plains, seemed to have the upper hand.   Gilgamesh, the spoiled and overbearing king, was about to be vanquished.   But evidently Gilgamesh hadn't ruled in Erech without realizing the importance of diplomacy. He brought his anger under control, fell on Enkidu's neck, and proclaimed him his friend.   From that moment on, Enkidu became Gilgamesh's constant companion, his counselor and servant.   Their friendship was the first in the history of heroic literature.   Like that of David and Jonathan, or Damon and Pythias, it was to lead them into many high adventures.

There are five Sumerian epics involving Gilgamesh, but two of them are so fragmentary they add little to the history of his exploits.   The Babylonian *Gilgamesh Cycle* was found inscribed on twelve clay tablets in Ashurbanipal's library at Nineveh. Ashurbanipal reigned in the seventh century B.C.   But the stories related on the tablets had their origins in the days when Gilgamesh was king in Erech.

The Babylonian tablets reveal their Sumerian sources in the names and places which play so large a part in the epics.   In recent years far older tablets have been unearthed, giving the Sumerian version of certain tales in the Gilgamesh legend. These were the originals from which the Babylonians concocted their versions, adding to them and changing them to suit their own political and religious viewpoints.

The Sumerian tales were composed long before they were actually written down on the clay tablets which have been unearthed and translated in the past hundred years. Minstrels sang of the exploits of Gilgamesh and Lugalbanda, both kings of Erech, decades before 2500 B.C., when the stories were first impressed on clay. These minstrels, accompanying their songs with harp or lyre, sang in the courts of kings to celebrate the adventures and achievements of their gods and the great heroes. The epics of Gilgamesh were favorites in those long ago times, which is perhaps one good reason why Gilgamesh is today the best known of Sumer's heroes.

Once Gilgamesh was subdued by Enkidu, as has been related, they were ready for the series of adventures that were to lead them to fame and glory. *Gilgamesh and Agga* is the shortest of the Sumerian epics concerning the hero, only 115 lines in length. But it tells a good deal about the constant struggle between the Sumerian city-states. From it we learn that Erech had a congress, a representative body, that debated the issues of the day.

At the start of the epic, Agga, the king of Kish, a city that had been foremost in importance in Sumer "since the Flood," was worried about the growing power of Erech. He sent an envoy to Gilgamesh to suggest that he submit to the overlordship of Kish or prepare for war. Gilgamesh was the last man to listen calmly to such demands. Instantly he got ready to take up arms against the haughty Agga. But first*

. . . the lord Gilgamesh before the elders of his city
Puts the matter, seeks out their word . . .
"Let us not submit to the house of Kish, let us smite
it with weapons."

*The translations of this and the following excerpts from the epics are those of Samuel Noah Kramer. For a full version of each one, see *The Sumerians*.

But the elders refused Gilgamesh's plea. They were in-
clined to knuckle under to the house of Kish. Angered by the
cowardice of these aged senators, Gilgamesh went before the
lower house of the assembly, the "men of his city." Perhaps
because they were younger and stronger of heart, this group
assumed a more warlike attitude. They decided to take up arms
against the house of Kish and "smite it with weapons." They
even went so far as to call Gilgamesh "the handiwork of the
gods" and a "king and hero." Much cheered by these expres-
sions of regard, Gilgamesh's "heart rejoiced, his spirit bright-
ened." He says to his servant Enkidu:

> Now then let the peaceful tool be put aside for
>   the violence of battle . . .
> He [Agga], when he comes—my great fear will
>   fall upon him. . . .

But unhappily for Gilgamesh's boast, "the days were not five,
the days were not ten" before Agga besieged Erech and "its
judgment was confounded." Undaunted, Gilgamesh rallied his
men and asked that "he who has heart let him arise, I would
have him go to Agga" to make a deal with the besieging forces.

One man named Birhurturre responded to the challenge and
"went out through the city gate." Instantly Birhurturre was
"seized." Then the soldiers of Kish "crush his flesh, bring him
before Agga."

Since Birhurturre had failed to impress Agga, Gilgamesh sent
another man outside the city gates and Agga asked of Birhurturre,

> Slave, is that man your king?
> That man is not my king, [said Birhurturre]
> Would that . . . were his strong forehead . . .
>   his bison-like face . . . his gracious fingers. . . .

At this response "the foreigners [the men of Kish] . . . felt not overwhelmed . . . bit not the dust."

Now Gilgamesh realized it was up to him to take charge and "ascended the wall . . . peered over the wall. . . ." When Agga saw him he again asked whether "that man [is] your king." When he heard that this was indeed the great Gilgamesh, "the multitude rolled in the dust . . . the lot of them felt overwhelmed." Agga, very wisely, "restrained his troops."

The very sight of the mighty Gilgamesh's "strong forehead" struck fear into the hearts of the men of Kish. But Gilgamesh felt he owed Agga something for "restraining his troops" and announced, "Agga, you have given me breath, you have given me life." Perhaps Gilgamesh was grateful that the reaction of the men of Kish influenced his own subjects in Erech and increased his stature in their eyes. In any case, the epic ends with a round of flowery compliments on both sides. As he lifted the siege, Agga extolled Gilgamesh as "king and hero, conqueror, prince beloved of An."

Every hero must slay his dragon, and Gilgamesh, like all the great heroes of history, had to perform this test of his powers. Later in Greek mythology, Hercules and Perseus met and conquered their own dragons, just as St. George did in Christian myth. But Gilgamesh was the first hero to meet this special challenge. The story is told in the second of the Gilgamesh epics, *Gilgamesh and the Land of the Living*. The tale has been pieced together from fourteen tablets and bits of inscribed clay, parts of which are lost or too obscure to be entirely clear. Like all Sumerian poetry it is repetitive, filled with high-sounding speeches and appeals to the gods, but, considered as imaginative drama, Professor Kramer calls it "one of the finest Sumerian literary works yet uncovered."*

The following is a selection of lines that give the bare bones of the story, leaving out the repetition and the more obscure passages:

*Samuel Noah Kramer, *History Begins at Sumer.*

In early Sumer religion inspired art such as this female idol of the Earth Mother, about 5000 BC. Museum of Aleppo.

The lord Gilgamesh sets his mind toward the "Land of the
    Living,"
He says to his servant Enkidu:
". . . I would enter the land, would set up my name . . .
Would raise up the names of the gods."
His servant Enkidu answers him:
"My master, if you would enter the land, inform Utu. . . ."
Gilgamesh says to the heavenly Utu:
"Utu, I would enter the land, be my ally . . .
In my city man dies, oppressed is the heart . . .
Man, the tallest, cannot reach to heaven,
Man, the widest, cannot cover the earth . . .
I would enter the land, would set up my name."
. . . Utu accepted his tears as an offering . . .
The lord Gilgamesh was overjoyed,
Mobilized his city like one man . . .
Single males who would do as he did, fifty, stood at his side.
He directed his step to the house of the smiths,
Forged the sword, the crushing ax, his "might of
    heaven" . . .
The sons of his city who accompanied him took them in their
    hands . . .
They crossed the first mountain. . . .

During their journey Gilgamesh and his "single males" climb
seven mountains, but fail to find the "cedar of his heart" until
they pass the seventh mountain. Gilgamesh instantly cuts it
down with his mighty ax and the faithful Enkidu chops off its
branches, which are then heaped into a pile. This activity
rouses the terrible monster Huwawa, who guards the cedar
tree. Unfortunately the text is destroyed at this point, but
evidently Huwawa, infuriated by this desecration of his cedar
tree, causes Gilgamesh to fall into a deep sleep. The text
becomes clear again as Enkidu tries to rouse him.

He speaks to him, he answers not . . .
Gilgamesh, lord, son of Kallub,

How long will you sleep?
The land has become dark, it is full of shadows . . .
Let not the sons of your city . . .
Stand waiting for you at the foot of the mountain.

Enkidu's words finally strike home to the sleeping Gilgamesh
and he

Raised himself on the great earth like a bull . . .
"Until I will have vanquished that fellow, whether he be a
    man . . . whether he be a god . . . I shall not turn
    to the city. . . ."
The faithful servant pleaded . . . "My master, you who have
    not seen that fellow are not terror-stricken,
. . . his teeth are a dragon's teeth,
His face is a lion's face. . . ."

But Gilgamesh refused to be intimidated by Enkidu's warn-
ings and encouraged his faithful friend by suggesting that they
"go forward together." Realizing he has little choice in the
matter, Enkidu agrees. They advance on the terrible monster
Huwawa, who has carefully "stayed close to his cedar house."
But Huwawa fixes Gilgamesh and his companion with "the eye
of death" and lets out such a terrible cry that even the mighty
Gilgamesh feels his sinews weaken and his feet tremble.
Although he was afraid, "he turned not back" and, with Enkidu
beside him, moved forward to face this fearsome creature.

Seven trees guarded the entrance to Huwawa's cedar house
and Gilgamesh, evidently realizing that these trees were
Huwawa's best defense, uprooted them one by one. The men
who accompanied him cut off the branches, bundled them up,
and placed them at the foot of the mountain. Now Gilgamesh
was free to approach the cedar house, where Huwawa awaited
him.

Apparently Huwawa made no attempt to defend himself, for
Gilgamesh

Pressed him [Huwawa] to his wall . . . slapped his cheek . . .
Tied a nose-ring on him, like a caught ox,
Fastened a rope about his arms like a caught warrior.
Huwawa—his teeth shook,
He clasped the lord Gilgamesh by the hand . . .
    groveled before him.
Then the princely Gilgamesh—his heart took pity on
    him. . . .

Gilgamesh suggests to Enkidu that they let Huwawa go free,
but Enkidu advises Gilgamesh not to be so generous. Obviously, he doesn't trust the dragon and says so in no uncertain
terms. This enrages Huwawa, who turns to Enkidu and says:

"Hired man, hungry, thirsty and obsequious,
Why did you speak ill of me to him!"
When he [Huwawa] had thus spoken,
Enkidu in his anger, cut off his neck,
Threw it into an arm-sack. . . .

Evidently hoping for the god Enlil's praise, Gilgamesh and
Enkidu bring Huwawa's severed head and place it before Enlil.
But when Enlil sees the head of the dragon, he becomes fu-
riously angry.

Why did you act thus!
Because you have laid hands on him . . .
May your faces be scorched,
May the food you eat be eaten by fire. . . .

Enlil's curse seems to doom Gilgamesh and Enkidu to a life
of wandering over the burning plains, but the epic becomes
obscure at this point and Gilgamesh's fate isn't at all clear.
In any case, he didn't find the eternal life for which he was
seeking in the cedar mountains. Enlil comforted him, however,

with a gift of seven *melams,* or divine rays, which must have helped him toward immortality, in literature if not in life.

The third of the Gilgamesh epics, *Gilgamesh, Enkidu and the Nether World,* has been pieced together from tablets, some of them found at Ur. A complete translation awaits further discovery of missing fragments, but the story as it stands shows Gilgamesh in a variety of roles, all of them very human indeed.

The first part of the poem deals with events that have little to do with Gilgamesh himself. It serves as a prologue to set the tone of the epic, as it emphasizes the powers of the gods in creating the world. Gilgamesh enters the story when the goddess Inanna asks his help. Apparently Inanna has tended a *huluppa* (willow) tree in her "fruitful garden," hoping, when it grew big, to use its wood to make a "fruitful throne for me to sit on." But as

> The tree grew big, its trunk bore no foliage,
> In its roots the snake who knows no charm set up its nest,
> In its crown the Imdugud-bird placed its young,
> In its midst the maid Lilith built her house . . .
> The maid Inanna—how she weeps!

The snake, the bird, and the vampire, Lilith, had stunted the tree and weeping Inanna decided to seek help from her brother, Utu, the sun god. But "as Utu came forth from the princely field" and listened to her woes,

> Her brother, the hero, the valiant Utu
> Stood not by her in this matter.

Depressed and still weeping because of Utu's ungallant response to her pleas, Inanna "speaks to the hero Gilgamesh." Like a true hero, Gilgamesh "stood by her in this matter."

> He donned armor weighing fifty minas about the waist . . .
> His ax of the road . . . he took in his hand,

At its roots he struck down the snake who knows no charm,
In its crown the Imdugud-bird took its young,
    climbed to the mountain,
In its midst the maid Lilith tore down her house,
    fled to the wastes.

As for the stunted tree, Gilgamesh, "plucked at its roots, tore
at the crown." The trunk he "gives it to the holy Inanna for
her throne." In gratitude Inanna "fashions its roots into a
pukku [drum] for him, fashions its crown into a *mikku* [drum-
stick] for him."

But Gilgamesh used the pukku and mikku to summon the
young men of Erech to war. ". . . in street and lane he made
the pukku resound . . ." and the men of Erech followed their
hero into battle. Later Gilgamesh took time to reflect on what
the drumming of his mikku had done. In every "street and

Demons such as this
one, may have
inhabited the nether
world of Gilgamesh.
Louvre.

lane" he "marked bitterness and woe! Captives! Dead! Widows!" Then, "because of the cry of the young maidens" and perhaps because the gods wanted to show Gilgamesh he had gone too far, "his pukku and mikku fell into the great dwelling place [the nether world]." When Gilgamesh tried to reach down into the nether world to recover them, he couldn't find either. So he sat down beside the great gate which led into the underworld and wept bitterly, calling for someone to help him bring his treasures up from the darkness below.

> Enkidu, his servant, says to him,
> My master, why do you weep?
> Why is your heart grievously sick?
> I will bring up your pukku from the nether world
> I will bring up your mikku from the "eye" of the nether
> world!

Gilgamesh instantly took Enkidu up on this offer, but felt he must first warn him about the dangers that will threaten him in this dismal nether world.

> Wear not clean clothes . . .
> Anoint not yourself with . . . sweet oil . . .
> Tie not sandals on your feet,
> Raise not a cry in the nether world . . .
> Lest the cry of the nether world hold you fast. . . .

But Enkidu, perhaps for the first time in the course of their friendship, "heeded not the word of his master." He wore clean clothes and anointed himself with oil. As a tragic result, Enkidu was caught fast in the nether world and was not able to return to Gilgamesh with the lost treasures.

Stricken with grief, Gilgamesh went to Nippur and tearfully appealed to Enlil for help. But "Father Enlil stood not by him in his matter." So Gilgamesh went on to the city of Eridu and appealed to Enki.

Father Enki stood by him in this matter,
Says to . . . the valiant Utu [the sun god] . . .
"Open now the vent of the nether world,
Raise Enkidu's ghost out of the nether world."
He [Utu] opened the vent of the nether world,
Raised Enkidu's ghost out of the nether world.
They [Gilgamesh and Enkidu] embrace . . . they sigh,
        they hold counsel:
"Tell me, what saw you in the nether world?"
"I will tell you, my friend, I will tell you."

But here the epic ends and Gilgamesh never learns what Enkidu had seen in the "land of the great beyond." And here the *Epic of Gilgamesh* ends, too.

With each passing year, as archaeologists, cryptographers, and Sumerologists study the clay tablets dug from Sumer's ancient sands, a deeper knowledge of this extraordinary civilization comes to light. The sculpture, trinkets, vases, and artifacts give some idea of Sumer's accomplishments. But the clay tablets tell the real story of the first civilization in the long, long story of mankind.

An inscription on a small bit of baked clay tells what Enki, to whom Sumer "must give praise in all things," thought of his creation:

Oh, Sumer, great land, of the lands of the universe,
Filled with steadfast light, dispensing from sunrise to sunset
        the divine laws to all the people,
Your divine laws are exalted laws, unreachable,
Your heart is profound, unfathomable,
The true learning which you bring . . . like heaven is untouchable . . .
Your lord is an honored lord; with An, the king, he sits on
        the heavenly dais,
Your king is the great mountain, the father Enlil . . .
May your steadfast temples lift hand to heaven. . . .

Suggested Reading

Beek, M. A. *Atlas of Mesopotamia.* Nelson and Sons, 1962. Fine maps, showing the archaeological sites.

Budge, Sir E. Wallis. *By Nile and Tigris.* John Murray, 1920. A vivid personal account of the author's explorations in Mesopotamia.

Chiera, E. *They Wrote on Clay.* 2nd. ed. Univ. of Chicago, 1955. A brief history of the author's explorations in the Near East, concentrating on the clay tablets and the work that has been done in translating them. Illustrated with pictures of sites and position maps.

Childe, V. G. *New Light on the Most Ancient Near East.* Grove Press, 1957. A brief review of the civilizations of Mesopotamia and surrounding areas.

Cottrell, Leonard. *Lost Worlds.* American Heritage Publishing Company, 1962. A picture history of the ancient civilizations with a special section devoted to each culture.

Cottrell, Leonard. *Quest for Sumer.* G. P. Putnam's Sons, 1965. A fascinating study of the early explorations, archaeological discoveries, art and architecture of the Sumerian civilization. Illustrated.

Frankfort, Henri. *The Art and Architecture of the Ancient Orient.* Penguin Books, 1955. Scholarly review of the early civilizations in Mesopotamia with special emphasis on art and architecture. Illustrated; maps.

Frankfort, Henri. *The Birth of Civilization in the Near East.* Anchor Books, 1950. A brief summary of the Mesopotamian civilizations.

Kramer, Samuel Noah. *History Begins at Sumer.* Anchor Books, 1959. The author shows striking evidence that some "firsts" in history were achieved by the Sumerians; the first bicameral congress, the first schools, the first "Farmers' Almanac," etc. Illustrated; maps.

Kramer, Samuel Noah. *The Sumerians.* Univ. of Chicago, 1963. Best general work on the Sumerians, their writing, laws and legend. Illustrated; maps.

Lloyd, Seton. *Art of the Ancient Near East.* Praeger, 1961. A beautifully illustrated volume, with an illuminating text.

Lloyd, Seton. *Twin Rivers.* Oxford University Press, 1943. A history of the "Land between the Rivers," the Tigris and Euphrates.

Moorgat, Anton. *The Art of Ancient Mesopotamia.* Phaidon [n.d.]. An English translation of a German classic.

Oppenheim, A. L. *Ancient Mesopotamia: Portrait of a Dead Civilization.* Univ. of Chicago, 1968. A very excellent general review of Mesopotamian cultural history.

Parrot, Andre. *Sumer.* Golden Press, 1961. The history of commercial development as well as a summary of the art and architecture of Sumer. Illustrated.

Pritchard, J. B., ed. *Ancient Near Eastern Texts.* Princeton University Press, 1955. Translations by many eminent scholars of the documents, inscriptions and clay tablets from these ancient peoples.

Woolley, Sir Leonard. *The Art of the Middle East.* Crown Publishers, 1961. The emphasis is on art, but the author includes many discussions of the social life, politics and commerce of these early civilizations.

Woolley, Sir Leonard. *Excavations at Ur.* Ernest Benn, Ltd., 1954. Moving narrative that gives a vivid idea of the labor involved in uncovering the past. Illustrated.

Woolley, Sir Leonard. *Ur of the Chaldees,* Penguin, 1929. A shorter account of the work done at Ur. Illustrated.

INDEX

DATE DUE